Culturally Sensitive Narrative Interventions for Immigrant Children and Adolescents

Giselle B. Esquivel
Geraldine V. Oades-Sese
Marguerite L. Jarvis

UNIVERSITY PRESS OF AMERICA,® INC.
Lanham • Boulder • New York • Toronto • Plymouth, UK

KH

Copyright © 2010 by
University Press of America,® Inc.
4501 Forbes Boulevard
Suite 200
Lanham, Maryland 20706
UPA Acquisitions Department (301) 459-3366

Estover Road
Plymouth PL6 7PY
United Kingdom

Library of Congress Control Number: 2009942543
ISBN: 978-0-7618-5034-2 (paperback : alk. paper)
eISBN: 978-0-7618-5035-9

⊗™ The paper used in this publication meets the minimum
requirements of American National Standard for Information
Sciences—Permanence of Paper for Printed Library Materials,
ANSI Z39.48-1992

1/21/11

To my children Daniel and Kristen, who were born in freedom and learned the stories of faith, courage, inner freedom, and peace.

Giselle B. Esquivel

In loving memory of my father, Severo "Bernie" Oades (1937-2009), whose musical, creative, and artistic legacy will live on. You are forever in my heart.

Geraldine V. Oades-Sese

I would like to thank my family and friends for their patience, understanding, and input during the evolution of my "Passion for Puppetry and Education." I would like to dedicate my contribution to the families and children, who, for whatever reason, find themselves in the challenging position of being "A Stranger in a Strange Land."

Marguerite L. Jarvis

Contents

Preface

The purpose of this book is to provide a scholarly perspective, integrating theory, research, and practical applications useful in the development and implementation of culturally sensitive narrative interventions for immigrant children and adolescents. This resource should prove of importance to counselors, school psychologists, educators, and other professionals working with culturally diverse children and families in educational or clinical settings. It may also be of interest and heuristic value to researchers involved in the study of culturally sensitive interventions. Moreover, it is expected that it serves as a useful instructional tool for graduate students preparing to provide services to children of diverse and immigrant backgrounds.

The authors were guided in writing this book by their professional academic and clinical expertise in the areas of multicultural psychology and education. They were motivated by their sensitivity to the needs of immigrant children based on their own personal stories as expressed below.

GISELLE

Why do I have to leave? This was one of the last questions I asked my mother before leaving Cuba in the early 60's, as she held me in her arms and comforted me on a rocking chair in a balcony facing the streets where we lived in Havana. This was a question heard over and over from Cuban children whose parents made a sacrificial choice to send them to the United States, either alone or with older siblings, in order to save them from the impending threats of communism.

Photo 1.   Giselle with a girl in Jamaica in 1961.

I was among those so called Peter Pan children who flew to this country at an early age, to find freedom in a land of hope and with the faith that a providential loving God would care for us. Thus began my journey on a flight to Jamaica (see Photo 1), holding on to my older brother Ruben, a young adolescent who for the time being was to be my protector.

The narratives of growing up years in the U.S. recount the stressors of every immigrant child, but also the joys of overcoming adversity. Growing up entails the ability, if not the effort, to integrate and bring meaning to our narrative journeys. We need each other along the way for we are all in some ways aliens and strangers in life coming together to share our stories. Yet, as storytellers (and wounded healers) we also need to listen to the voices of children tell broken tales, and to help them find healing in the creative expression and recreation of their life stories.

Looking back at my early years in Cuba, I find my source of resilience in the stories of childhood in a bilingual Methodist school and church which laid the foundation for my academic and spiritual journeys. Amidst the losses, images begin to appear of playful friends...dancing dreams...make believe games...the rhythm of poems...creative imaginings...fairy tale plays...and the natural freedom of being a child...all remain with me still. Most of all, time brings back memories of that Peter Pan girl who was held by her mother; whose answer to my question showed me the way of faith, courage, and the true meaning of freedom.

GERALDINE

A picture is truly worth a thousand words. I was very fortunate to happen upon a photograph (see Photo 2) which captured the most singular event that would change my life; the turning point from which all experiences that followed would transpire into the fuel of my career. In 1973, my father, Bernie, sister, Bernadette and I journeyed to the United States with hope for a better life. Formally attired, it was customary for Filipinos to dress up when traveling

Photo 2. My father, Bernie, younger sister, Bernadette, and I (right) boarding on a plane to the United States in 1973.

to the U.S. because it was considered a special privilege to fly. My father is seen wearing an *Americana* (the Tagalog word for a suit), while my sister and I were adorned with new dresses and hand-made leis of jasmine around our necks. I emigrated to the U.S. from the Philippines at the age of 5. Like some immigrant families, one parent would usually travel ahead to find a stable job and home before sending for their family. In my case, my mother left Manila to seek employment in the U.S. as a dentist. She left my father, sister, and me with my grandparents; and we then followed her a year later.

When I first arrived in the U.S., I was surprised to see that television shows were in color and that there were many cartoons to watch besides the black and white versions of *Popeye* and *Felix the Cat* that were shown in the Philippines at the time. Apart from the excitement and anxiety that most immigrants feel, I also felt sad because I missed my grandparents who we left behind in the Philippines.

I also remember how difficult it was not to understand or speak English, and the prejudice that my family experienced. It was particularly difficult in school. The language barrier made me feel less competent than the other children because, unlike me, they were proficient in English. I remember feeling certain camaraderie with my Hispanic classmates because, essentially, we were in the same situation. I also remember wishing to gain the affection and attention of the teacher, which other children were able to easily attain. In retrospect, however, I do consider myself fortunate to have grown up in the very culturally diverse community of Jersey City, New Jersey. The diverse demographics made adjusting to a new country slightly easier- it was a protective factor for me. That is not to say, however, that I escaped prejudice and inequity altogether. As a child, I never understood why people saw me as "different" from themselves based on the way I looked. Other children would say terrible things such as "Go back to China" while slanting their eyes with their fingers to mock me. I remember thinking to myself that I was Filipino, not Chinese, and wondered what was wrong with that?

I remember feeling lost in school and embarrassed when I tried to pronounce words. Math was easier, except when there were word problems. One particular memory, I shall never forget. In first grade, the teacher asked the class if anyone knew the vowels of the alphabet. Feeling excited and confident, I held up my hand and was called on to answer. I quickly replied, "/a/, /e/, /i/, /o/, and /u/", instead of the standard letter naming of a, e, i, o, u. And so, enthusiasm quickly turned into shock and fear upon seeing the look on my teacher's face and giggles from my classmates. After being taken aback by my unconventional response, she corrected me and stated the letter names of vowels. I felt so embarrassed. In the Philippines, children recited the alphabet and vowels by their letter sounds rather than by their letter names because it was considered a practical foundation for learning how to read. Needless to say, I was left wishing to be as smart as the other students. My grades were atrocious, receiving Cs and Ds, until I reached the fourth grade. It was because of a very caring, patient, dedicated, and persistent third grade teacher, who decided to help me after school, that my grades began to improve. It was because of this wonderful teacher, Ms. Woolichuck (I still remember her name and face to this day) that I started getting straight A's the following year from 4th grade on and ultimately graduated as Valedictorian in 8th grade. Hence, it is important to allow immigrant children enough time and guidance to adjust to their new environment after being uprooted and replanted on foreign soil.

Exploring my ethnic identity and heritage occurred later in my life. It was not until graduate school with the help of my mentor, Dr. Giselle Esquivel that I finally accepted my cultural background and heritage and instilled a life-long career interest in helping children from culturally and linguistically diverse backgrounds. I struggled, and still continue to struggle, with my ethnic identity because of the terrible prejudice, bias, and inequity that I faced throughout my life. These negative feelings that I buried deep within my subconscious did not resurface until they were revealed through a required project for Dr. Joseph Ponterotto's multicultural course at Fordham University.

The importance of understanding the experiences of immigrant children, adolescents, and families is crucial to helping them succeed. Children need a safe haven or a way of expressing their feelings of depression, anxiety, inequity, discrimination, and isolation. The process of acculturation takes time. Interventions that serve immigrant children and adolescents are much needed. These interventions must be culturally sensitive; allow for expression of negative and positive experiences; foster growth; and develop caring and culturally competent teachers, psychologists, and other school staff. Therefore, my experiences as an immigrant child and mentorship by Giselle Esquivel have led me to study the resilience of children from culturally and linguistically diverse backgrounds and develop culturally salient interventions to foster their success.

Cristina Igoa (2003) states very eloquently the importance of supporting immigrant children and allowing them the time to adjust and thrive- becoming resilient:

> Even though immigrant children have left behind their systems of communication, their cultural beliefs, and the cultural identity that once gave meaning to their lives, the psychological traumas of uprooting are less visible and less easily measured than their language proficiency...This culture shock is much as the same as the shock we observe in a plant when a gardener transplants it to one

soil to another…Some plants survive, often because of the gardener's care; some children survive because of a teacher, peers, or a significant person who nurtures them during the transition toward integration into a new social milieu (p. 39).

PEG

As a young child I experienced both sides of foreign language acquisition, and expressive language issues. A native English speaker, I lived in Thailand (see Photo 3) from the age of six to nine, with my parents, while my father was on sabbatical from Rutgers. I had to rapidly assimilate the local language (Thai), interpreting for my mother as she taught puppetry and social skills at the Bangkok School for the Deaf, (as well as shopping in the local markets). My emerging "Passion for Puppets" led to my current interest in using puppetry in educational, clinical, and therapeutic venues. It has been a real "eye-opener" to share some of the things that happened to me as a child . . . those events have left real scars. I believe that my experiences created an appreciation for being "outside – looking in" and have helped me empathize with, and

Photo 3.   Peggy and her parents and friend on the beach on the coast of Thailand, in 1954.

seek out, minority children with similar issues. During my teaching career, I observed how reticent and non-vocal ELL students could express themselves and acquire language through the use of puppets. These observations led me to use these strategies with multicultural students of immigrant background. In addition, teaching in a bilingual school in New Jersey, working with ELL children in Vermont, and working with children from many countries, gave me a real appreciation for the complex issues that surround children of immigrant background, both in school and at home. Working with parent groups, and meeting with families to work out difficult issues, helped fuel enthusiasm for helping these immigrant families adjust to new environments, languages, and cultures, while still maintaining language, culture and family values, from their countries of origin.

Acknowledgments

We would like to extend our sincere gratitude to Dan McAdams for taking the time to provide a wonderful commentary for our book.

We would also like to acknowledge Richard Andrew Sese for his artistic creativity and graphical skills in designing the front cover of our book.

Special thanks to Lonnie Miller for her editorial expertise in reviewing the book.

We acknowledge the help from our Rutgers doctoral students: Matt Robinson, Chris Velderman, and Kaitlin Gonzales for their help with correcting the proofs and creating the index.

Chapter One

Culturally-Linguistically Diverse and Immigrant Children: Stressors of Migration and the Acculturation Process

CULTURALLY DIVERSE CHILDREN AND ADOLESCENTS

The demographic composition of the United States is continually changing as a result of the significant population increase of culturally-linguistically diverse (CLD) immigrant children and their families. While immigrant children account for 20 percent of all children in the U.S., their numbers are growing at a faster rate than the mainstream populations of children (Child Trends, 2007). It is estimated that in about 20 years, 48 percent of U.S. adolescents will be from racial and ethnic minority backgrounds. Immigrant children originate from many countries and have settled across the 50 states. The majority of children are from Mexico (40 percent) and the remaining 60 percent come from the Caribbean, East Asia, Europe, Central America, South America, Indochina (i.e., Cambodia, Laos, Thailand, and Vietnam), West Asia, the former Soviet Union, and Africa (see Figure 1.1). Children from Arab immigrant families, however, are not represented in the U.S. Census because they are considered White (Haboush, 2007). The largest percentage of Arab Americans is Lebanese Christians, followed by Egyptians and Syrians (Brittingham & de la Cruz, 2005; de la Cruz & Brittingham, 2003). Iraqis and Moroccans make up the largest numbers of recent arrivals. Most Arab Americans are 2nd and 3rd generation; however, more recent immigrants to the United States have entered in response to the Gulf War and War on Iraq.

Hispanics are the largest culturally diverse population in the United States (U.S. Census Bureau, 2009) and they are growing at a faster rate than any other immigrant group (Casas & Vasquez, 1996; Clemente & Collison, 2000; Garcia & Marotta, 1997; Zapata, 1995). Child Trends (2007) indicates that children of Mexican descent account for 50-81 percent of children from immigrant families in 12 states, including several states in the West (Arizona,

Immigration Statistics

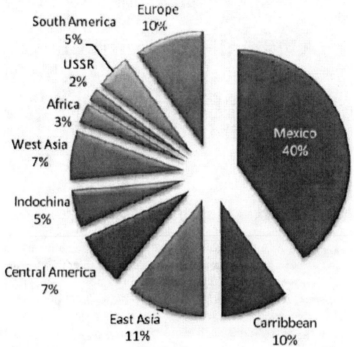

**Figure 1.1.   Percentage of children from immigrant families in the U.S.
Source: Child Trends (2007).**

California, Colorado, Idaho, Nevada, and New Mexico), the South (Arkansas, Oklahoma, and Texas), and the Midwest (Illinois, Kansas, Nebraska). The largest proportions of children from immigrant families of 14 states originated from Europe, Canada, and Australia. East Asians make up the largest proportions of immigrant children in Alaska, Hawaii, Maryland, and Virginia. Caribbean immigrants constitute the greater proportions in Florida, New Jersey, and New York. Families from Indochinese backgrounds have settled in Louisiana and Minnesota, while Central American families have settled in the District of Columbia and West Asian families in Michigan.

Sixty-eight percent of children of immigrants have lived in the U.S. 10 years or more, including 24 percent with parents who were born in the United States. Only 21 percent of children of immigrants lived in the U.S. less than 10 years. The majority (79 percent) of children from immigrant families are American citizens (Child Trends, 2007).

A number of immigrant children are refugees. In fact, more than half of the refugee groups are comprised of children (United Nations Higher Commission for Refugees, 2008). Both refugee and voluntary immigrant children share similar characteristics in terms of difficulties experienced in learning a new language, acculturating to a new country, and adjusting to the school environment of the host culture. Refugee children are considered to be involuntary immigrants, fleeing their native country as a result of political- or war-related circumstances. In the 1980s, 85 percent of refugees came from Latin America. In 2002, refugees with legal status were from Bosnia-Herzegovina, Cuba, Iran, Afghanistan, Ukraine, and Sudan. Altogether, the greatest number of refugee children came from Somalia, Ethiopia, and Liberia (Office of Immigration Statistics, 2008). After the 1990s, refugees came from Afghanistan, Bosnia, Iraq, Burundi, Sudan, and Somalia (U.S. Committee for Refugees and Immigrants, 2008). Approximately 53,000 refugees were admitted in 2004. The largest minority of refugee school-age children, including those of illegal immigrant status, is of Latino/Hispanic background and it is predicted that they will constitute 25 percent of the school population by 2030.

The educational experience and performance of immigrant students depend upon multiple factors that include: (1) age on arrival, (2) previous schooling, (3) home language, (4) literacy, (5) family education and aspirations, (6) economic circumstances, (7) immigration status, and (8) current level of English language proficiency. Moreover, the adjustment of immigrant children to the host school environment is often predicated on the level of responsiveness of the host school to their learning needs and social emotional stressors.

SOURCES OF STRESS FOR CLD
IMMIGRANT CHILDREN AND ADOLESCENTS

Children of immigrant background experience a number of stressors related to their initial migration experience: the negative effects of poverty, language and learning adjustment issues, and the overall process of acculturation. The study of stress among immigrant and refugee children is limited since most attention has been given to research on adults. Nonetheless, studies on immigrant children suggest that stress has a negative impact on their social-emotional and academic adjustment. Higher rates of violence exposure leading to posttraumatic stress disorder have been found among immigrant and refugee children (Arroyo & Eth, 1996; Guarnaccia & Lopez, 1998; Jaycox et. al., 2002), while a number of problems related to migration stress are manifested as identity and behavioral disorders (Aronowitz, 1984; Garcia Coll & Magnuson, 1997). Family disruption is another major risk factor for immigrant children (e.g., Suarez-Orozco & Suarez-Orozco, 2001) along with the loss of support from extended family members.

MIGRATION EXPERIENCES
AMONG CLD CHILDREN AND ADOLESCENTS

A number of stressors have been associated with different stages of migration (Gonsalves, 1992). Preflight experiences may involve a sense of helplessness over political events and circumstances of risk in the country of origin. Refugees report heightened feelings of anxiety and a sense of abandonment upon leaving their country of origin (Keller, 1975). Children may experience anticipatory anxiety and confusion dependent on the reasons for migration. Involuntary immigrants may have experienced civil war, homelessness, lack of formal education, exposure to violence, and the witnessing of killings of relatives or members of their family (Hones & Cha, 1999; Laosa, 1990; Suarez-Orozco & Suarez-Orozco, 2001; Suarez-Orozco & Todorova, 2003; Tollefson, 1989). A sense of impending danger is another characteristic of refugee migration. In contrast, voluntary immigrants and refugees who can plan their departure and flight may have developed second language abilities, tend to be better educated, have a set of vocational skills, and enjoy greater financial resources (Kunz, 1972; Rumbaut & Portes, 2001).

The flight phase itself may convey trauma dependent on its circumstances and level of intensity and duration (Kunz, 1972). For example, Cuban children in the first wave of migration, referred to as the "Peter Pan" generation, often came to the U.S. alone or with older siblings and lived in foster homes until reunited with their parents. The second waves of children refugees from Cuba and Vietnam, known as "boat people" or rafters were usually poorer, faced greater danger, were often unaccompanied by parents, and risked their lives at sea (Kunz; Zhou, 2001). Children of families who are of undocumented status by crossing borders illegally face similar immediate risks, along with more long-term consequences, such as limited health services and possible fear of being identified and deported.

The process of resettlement itself can be divided into stages of (1) early arrival characterized by some disorientation, sadness, and anger. Children may experience trauma as a result of loss of family ties, disruption of friendships, and social instability (Boyden de Berry, Feeny, & Hart, 2002; Esquivel & Keitel, 1990); (2) experimentation and stabilization, and (3) normalization or decompensation. Migration experiences may lead to significant psychological distress including alienation from school peers, and lowered self-esteem (Kao, 1999; Portes & Rumbaut, 1996).

Overall, circumstances around migration, characteristics of the migrant family, the nature of the host community and its support system (Guarnaccia and Lopez, 1998), and the interplay of other social and individual factors influence the adjustment of children. The socioeconomic status of immigrant families is also a critical factor in determining the extent of exposure to stressful life situations (Huyck & Fields, 1981; Perez, 2001).

EFFECTS OF POVERTY

Twenty-five percent of children of low socioeconomic background in the U.S. are immigrants or children of immigrants (Capps, Fix, & Reardon-Anderson, 2003). Most children of immigrants (51 percent) live in families with incomes below the poverty level. Unlike children of U.S. born parents, immigrant children experience significantly greater hardships and are less likely to receive public benefits that could enhance their health status and psychological well-being (Greenberg & Rhamanou, 2004). U.S. workforce policies deny immigrant parents the help they need to move beyond the low-wage labor market (Greenberg & Rhamanou). Immigrant children are more likely to live in crowded homes, have poor health, and are unable to afford food and basic needs (Fass & Cauthen, 2006; Nightingale & Fix, 2004). These problems are not the result of unemployment, but stem primarily from low-wages, limited English proficiency, and low-level education. Furthermore, racial and ethnic stereotypes of immigrants result in public ambivalence toward funding policies related to poverty (Kaufmann & Lay, 2004).

Recent statistics further support the portrayal of hardship experienced by America's poor children. Fass and Cauthen (2006) indicated that in 2005, 26% of children of immigrant families were poor, compared to16% of children of native-born parents. California, Florida, Illinois, New Jersey, New York, and Texas have the largest immigrant population with the poverty rate among children of immigrant parents ranging from 14% to 40%. These children are at risk for poor cognitive, academic, physical, and social-emotional development (Garcia Coll et al., 1996; McLoyd, 1998). From an ecological perspective, development is "profoundly affected (indirectly) by the child's social position within a socially-stratified society replete with racism and discrimination" (p. 82, Garcia Coll & Szalacha, 2004). This is further exacerbated by limited language proficiency and stressors related to immigration and acculturation. Moreover, Hernandez (2004) found parental education level as a significant determinant of children's well-being and development. Higher levels of education offer opportunities for better jobs, adequate living conditions, healthcare, resources, and social status.

Despite the adversities related to poverty and the acculturation process, some immigrant families hold a repository of strengths which makes them resilient. These strengths include good health; strong work ethics; and access to community of immigrants that help the transition to a new country (Hernandez, 2004). Moreover, programs that target families and their young children (i.e., Early Head Start) have been shown to improve children's cognitive and social-emotional development, as well as enhance parenting skills (Fass & Cauthen, 2006). High-quality early childhood experiences help close the achievement gap between poor and well-off children.

SECOND LANGUAGE LEARNING

Another major challenge that affects immigrant children and refugees is learning a second language—English—in addition to adapting to a new culture. More than half of immigrant children have at least one parent in the home who speaks English exclusively or fluently, with the exception of California. Seventy-five percent of children from immigrant families speak English exclusively or fluently, while 46% are bilingual (Child Trends, 2007). However, 25% of children live in linguistically isolated homes. Children who are limited in English proficiency are faced with many challenges when they enter the school system that is ill-prepared to educate them. Generally, learning basic interpersonal communication skills (BICS) in English takes about 2 to 5 years and learning English required for academic success (CALP) takes about 5 to 7 years (Cummins, 1981). Lack of understanding the differences between BICS and CALP has resulted in the overrepresentation of CLD children in special education presumably as a result of behavioral and learning difficulties (Artiles, Palmer, & Trent, 2004).

Immigrant parents often equate success for their children with the ability to speak English exclusively, at the risk of losing their native language along with their cultural values (Mushi, 2002). A contributing factor to this misperception is the status of the minority language placed by the American culture. This approach toward "subtractive bilingualism" is counterintuitive and has been shown to result in negative developmental outcomes such as low academic achievement. Furthermore, losing the native language creates social distance between generations (Silverstein & Chen, 1999). In contrast "additive bilingualism"—mastering the native language while gaining proficiency in English—has shown to have cognitive (Peal & Lambert, 1962) and social-emotional advantages (Oades-Sese & Esquivel, 2006).

Bilingual children outnumber children of immigrant families with limited English proficiency in every state (except South Dakota). Therefore, these children are well-positioned to become fluent bilinguals (i.e., speaking, reading, and writing), if they receive formal training in both English and the native language of their parents (Child Trends, 2007). Effective schools for English Language Learners (ELL) include (a) the value placed on the linguistic and cultural background of ELL students, (b) high expectations for achievement, and (c) parental involvement in the overall functions of the school environment (Verdugo & Flores, 2007).

Academic underachievement and poor school performance is another concern. In particular, Latino students have the highest school drop-out rate than any other group in the U.S. (Casas & Vasquez, 1996; Dana, 1998; Fracasso & Busch-Rossnagel, 1992; Garcia & Marotta, 1997; Santiago-Rivera, 1995). On the other end, children from Asian cultural groups (e.g., Korean) experience family pressures to excel academically (Terzini-Hollar, 2008).

EFFECTS OF THE ACCULTURATION PROCESS

Acculturation is defined as a process of change experienced by an individual or group from another culture coming into contact with a host culture (Berry, Poortinga, Segall, & Dansen, 2002). Psychological acculturation is referred to the experiences of an individual (in this case a child) to develop a sense of belonging, self-esteem, academic success, ethnic identity, and overall identity development. Sociological acculturation refers to the social changes and adaptation experiences of the social group as a whole to new social, geographic conditions, economic, and political structures. Group experiences of cultural congruence with the host culture, how members are received, how the culture is regarded, and how they are prepared to fit in, are sources of support for the cultural group (Ogbu, 1982). In turn, the socio-cultural adjustment of the group and parents serves as positive community and family support systems for children (Nahari, Martines, & Marquez, 2007).

There are different types of acculturation processes: (a) *Integration* involves adopting the values, beliefs, and behaviors of the host culture, while retaining those of the native culture, (b) *Separation* involves retaining the native culture and resisting adaptation to the host culture, (c) *Assimilation* is the process of adopting the host culture and forgoing the native culture, and (d) *Marginalization* involves no affiliation with either the host or native cultures. Stressors related to marginalized acculturation often lead to depression, anxiety, psychosomatic symptoms, and identity problems (Berry & Kim, 1988; Hovey & King, 1996; Williams & Berry, 1991).

School-aged children are particularly vulnerable to the challenges of coordinating two cultures and languages, potentially creating psychological and behavioral problems (Tong, Huang, & McIntyre, 2006). Rates of acculturation to the mainstream society may differ between parents and their children. Children often acculturate at a faster rate than their parents due to more extensive opportunities to engage with peers in school (Ying & Han, 2007). Differences in level of acculturation result in a process called *dissonant acculturation* (Portes & Rumbaut, 1996) or create "intergenerational discrepancy" (Ying & Han, 2007). Children of immigrants tend to acquire English faster, adopt the values and lifestyle of the American culture, and form cross-racial relationships more readily than older family members- potentially leading to feelings of alienation and conflicts with their parents (Lee et al., 2000; Szapocznik et al., 1984). Although conflicts are part of the normal process of acculturation, failure to resolve these differences can result in behavioral problems (Vega, Khoury, Zimmerman, Gil, & Warheit, 1995), low self-esteem (Gil, Vega, & Dimas, 1994), and conduct disorder (Szapocznik et al.).

Adolescent immigrants may perceive significant conflicts with families as a result of acculturation gaps or differential rates of acculturation across generations (Delgado-Gaitan, 2004; Portes & Rumbaut, 2001; Zhou & Bankston, 1998). Generational conflicts and identity development disruptions or arrests may occur (Zhou & Bankston; Zhou, 2001). Adolescents confronting these conflicts may show more oppositional, aggressive, destructive, and antisocial behaviors (Lau et al., 2005).

Marginalized parents and/or children lead to greater risks of children's conduct problems. This is consistent with previous research that marginalization is associated with feelings of alienation and depression. For Mexican American high-risk families, highly acculturated fathers and their adolescents reported more conflict than less acculturated fathers (Lau et al., 2005). Less acculturated family members appear more invested in preserving harmonious and respectful relationships with one another and are less accepting of open expressions of conflict, whereas more acculturated families tend to value direct communication, which may result in more open expression of conflicts (Flores, Tschann, VanOss Marin, & Pantoja, 2004). Recent research has shown that acculturation levels of mothers impact family processes regardless of mother-child acculturation discrepancies (Dumka, Roosa, & Jackson, 1997; Gonzales, Deardorff, Barr, Formosa, & Barrera, 2005).

Regarding South Asian families, involuntary migrants or refugees are less prepared for the move and may also be less able or willing to acculturate to American culture, thereby increasing the intergenerational gap (Ying & Han, 2007). This is further exacerbated by the differences between Southeast Asian and American cultures. Southeast Asian cultures value family over the individual, respect the elderly over the young, and embrace lifelong obligations to the family of origin (Ying & Chao, 1996). Intergenerational discrepancy has predicted negative outcomes among Southeast Asian American adolescents, including school difficulties (Yao, 1985), depression (Wong, 2001), gang involvement (Zhou & Bankston, 1998), and suicidality (Lau, Jernewall, Zane, & Myers, 2002). Ying and Han have found that girls reported more depressive symptom than boys, possibly because they ruminate more over problems and feel less in control of their lives. In Korean American and other Asian families stress is also created by a strong emphasis on academic achievement and acceptance into elite colleges based on individual effort, without an understanding of some of the admission practices (e.g., geographic representation quotas) of higher education institutions.

Bosnian and Muslim immigrants and refugee children also face significant acculturation pressures and experience intergenerational discrepancy between parent and child (Mayadas & Segal, 2000). This may be further exacerbated by the attacks of 9-11 in New York City and the Pentagon resulting in xenophobic based attitudes from American peers (Synder, May, Zulcic, & Gabbard, 2005). Furthermore, these families are faced with the fact that their religion, Islam, may not be viewed positively or as one that contributes to a pluralistic multicultural nation (Yazbeck-Haddad & Esposito, 2000).

Arab families have immigrated to the U.S. in response to the Gulf War, Iraq-Iran War, and the War in Iraq complicating their adjustment and acculturation to the U.S. (Haboush, 2007). The terrorist attack on September 11, 2001 has further contributed to negative perceptions of the Arab culture, resulting in bullying of Arab children (Abdelkarim, 2003). Nonetheless, relative to those of other immigrants, average levels of education and family income are higher for Arab Americans, which may facilitate assimilation faster (Brittingham & de la Cruz, 2005). Religion in Arab culture influences family life, child rearing, and views regarding education and psychology (Haboush). Muslims have more difficulty assimilating than Arab Christians because the latter identify more with Western culture.

EFFECT OF ACCULTURATION DIFFERENCES OF SIBLINGS

Acculturative patterns of siblings are also important considerations to understanding adaptation among immigrant families. Pyke (2005) examined the acculturative differences among siblings and its impact on family dynamics-particularly among Japanese and Vietnamese immigrant families. Siblings of immigrant families can play an important role in shaping one another's acculturative process. They can reinforce native cultural practices through example and teachings or introduce one another to aspects of the mainstream culture (e.g., new ideas, language, styles of dressing, and friends). The oldest sibling often assumes parentified roles, such as caring for, disciplining, and teaching younger siblings the values and beliefs of their native culture. Older children are pressured to comply with parental rules and cultural practices compared to younger children. Parents' differential expectations and treatment of older and younger children provide a better explanation of siblings' acculturative dissimilarities. Birth order has also been shown to affect different sets of expectations, tasks, and statuses for the oldest and youngest child in a family (Cicirelli, 1995); with first-borns, particularly in Asian families, having higher status and authority. The oldest child is typically given more responsibilities binding him/her more tightly to the cultural traditions than younger siblings who are freer to engage and be influenced by the mainstream culture (Pyke). First-borns regularly help parents with financial matters and language translation- leading to better fluency of native language.

Although the role of disciplinarian and cultural preservationist provides the oldest sibling with power and authority, it undermines sibling solidarity (Pyke, 2005). *Assimilated or more acculturated siblings are viewed as "black sheeps" of the family.* This is an example from Pyke's study:

> Whereas So-Jung embraces her Korean culture and identity, Lily rejects it and claims an American identity. So-Jung said about Lily, She speaks English all the time. It's like she is ashamed of speaking our language. She will say, "Speak English, we are in America, not Korea." Even at family gatherings, she will speak to everyone in English, and my family gets really annoyed. She hardly interacts with the rest of my family because they are real cultural. They labeled my sis the black sheep in our family. I feel resentment toward her because she will not let my culture be a part of her life, which makes me feel she does not want to be associated with my parents or me. And that really hurts. (p. 509)

PARENTIFIED ROLES AND LANGUAGE BROKERING

As part of the acculturation process, children become communicative liaisons between their parents and the community and transmitters of cultural knowledge to their families (Suarez-Orozco & Suarez-Orozco, 2001; Weisskirch, 2006). Children serve as translators during face-to-face or telephone discussions and as interpreters of letters, and other documents. This process is called *language brokering*. Among immigrant Mexican families, children serve as language brokers, tutors, and surrogate parents in the course of acculturation (Valenzuela, 1999), a process that may be very stressful. However, De Ment, Muriel, and Villanueva (2005) have found that Latino and Asian American college students view language brokering as a way to gain empathy and compassion for their parents, despite feelings of obligation and annoyance. Consistent with this positive view, language brokering is beneficial in gaining sophisticated communication and decision-making skills (De Ment et al.), independence and maturity among Latino high school students (Tse, 1995), higher-self-esteem (Weisskirch), and academic performance and self-efficacy (Buriel et al., 1998). A positive attitude toward language brokering may result in a greater sense of ethnic identity (Weisskirch, 2005). A negative consequence of assuming parentified roles by children is that assuming too much authority and adult-like responsibilities at an early age can disrupt the normal development process (Umana-Taylor, 2003).

In sum, CLD and immigrant children are exposed to a series of stressors that form part of the migration experience and acculturation process. These stressors have the potential of resulting in mental health problems and adjustment difficulties in the absence of protective factors and sources of support and resources.

REFERENCES

Abdelkarim, R. Z. (2003, May). Arab and Muslim Americans: Collateral damage in the wars on terrorism, Iraq. *Washington Report on Middle East Affairs, 22,* 55–56.

Aronowitz, M. (1984). The social and emotional adjustment of immigrant children. International Migration Review, 26, 89–110.

Arroyo, W., & Eth, S. (1996). Post-traumatic disorder and other stress reactions. In R. J. Apfel & B. Simon (Eds.), Minefields in their hearts: The mental health of children in war and communal violence (pp. 52–74). New Haven, CT: Yale University Press.

Artiles, A. J., Trent, S. C., & Palmer, J. (2004). Culturally diverse students in special education: Legacies and prospects. In J.A. Banks & C.M. Banks (Eds.), Handbook of research on multicultural education (2nd ed., pp. 716–735). San Francisco, CA: Jossey Bass.

Berry, J. W., & Kim, U. (1988). Acculturation and mental health. In P. Dasen, J. W. Berry, & N. Sartorius (Eds.), Health and cross-cultural psychology: Towards applications (pp. 207–238). Newbury Park, CA: Sage.

Berry, J. W., Poortinga, Y. H., Segal, M. H., & Dansen, P. R. (2002). *Cross-cultural psychology: Research and applications* (2nd ed.). New York: Cambridge University Press.

Boyden, J, Berry, J, Feeny, T., & Hart, J. (2002). Children affected by conflict in South Asia: A review of trends and issues identified through secondary research. Refugee Studies Centre, RSC Working Paper No. 7, University of Oxford. Retrieved May 27, 2008, from *http://www.rsc.ox.ac.uk/PDFs/workingpaper7.pdf*

Brittingham, A., & de la Cruz, G. P. (2005). *We the people of Arab ancestry in the United States: Census 2000 special reports.* Washington, DC: U.S. Census Bureau.

Buriel, R., Perez, W., De Ment, T. L., Chavez, D. V., & Moran, V. R. (1998). Hispanic Journal of Behavioral Sciences, 20(3), 283–297.

Capps, R., Fix, M., & Reardon-Anderson, J. (2003, November) *Children of immigrants show slight reductions in poverty, hardship.* Washington, DC: Urban Insti-
tute. Retrieved May 27, 2008, from http://www.urban.org/urlprint.cfm?ID=8641.

Casas, J. M., & Vasquez, M. J. T. (1996). Counseling the Hispanic: A guiding frame-
work for a diverse population. In P. B. Pederson, J. D. Draguns, W. J. Lonner, &
J. E. Trimble (Eds.), Counseling across cultures (4th ed., pp. 146–176). Thousand
Oaks, CA: Sage.

Child Trends (2007). Children in Immigrant Families. Retrieved May 27, 2008, from
http://www.childtrends.org/Files//Child_Trends-2007_04_01_TBL_ChildrenIn-
ImmigrantFamilies.pdf

Cicirelli, V. G. (1995). *Sibling relationships across the life span.* New York: Plenum
Press.

Clemente, R., & Collison, B. (2000). The relationships among counselors, ESL teachers, and students. *Professional School Counseling, 3*(5), 339.

Cummins, J. (1981). The role of primary language development in promoting educational success for language minority students. In Schooling and language minority students: A theoretical framework (pp. 3–49). Los Angeles: California State
University; Evaluation, Dissemination, and Assessment Center. Retrieved May
5, 2008, from http://www.eric.ed.gov/ERICDocs/data/ericdocs2sql/content_stor-
age_01/0000019b/80/2e/a8/84.pdf

Dana, R. H. (1998). *Understanding cultural identity in intervention.* Thousand Oaks,
CA: Sage Publications.

de la Cruz, G. P., & Brittingham, A. (2003). *The Arab Population: 2000.* (Census 2000
Brief No. C2KBR-23). U.S. Department of Commerce, U.S. Census Bureau.

De Ment, T. L., Buriel, R., & Villanueva, C. M. (2005) Children as language brokers: A
narrative of the recollections of college students. In R. Hoosain & F. Salili (Eds.) *Language in Multicultural Education* (pp. 255_272). Greenwich, CT: Information Age.

Delgado-Gaitan, C. (2004). *Involving Latino families in schools: raising student achievement through home-school partnerships.* Thousand Oaks, CA: Corwin Press.

Dumka, L. E., Roosa, M. W., & Jackson, K. M. (1997). Risk, conflict, mothers' parenting, and children's adjustment in low-income, Mexican immigrant, and Mexican American families. Journal of Marriage and the Family, 59, 309–323.

Esquivel, G. B., & Keitel, M. A. (1990). Counseling immigrant children in the
schools. Elementary School Guidance & Counseling, 24, 213–221.

Fass, S., & Cauthen, N. K. (2006). *Who are America's Poor Children?: The Official
Story.* National Center for Children in Poverty, Columbia Mailman School of Public
Health. Retrieved July 1, 2008, from http://nccp.org/publications/pub_684.html

Flores, E., Tschann, J. M., VanOss Marin, B., & Pantoja, P. (2004). Marital conflict
and acculturation among Mexican American husbands and wives. Cultural Diversity and Ethnic Minority Psychology, 10, 39–52.

Fracasso, M. P., & Busch-Rossnagel, N. A. (1992). Parents and children of Hispanic
origin. In M. E. Procidano & C. B. Fisher (Eds.), Contemporary families: A handbook for school professionals (pp. 83–98). New York: Teachers College Press.

Garcia, J., & Marotta, S. (1997). Characterization of the Latino population. In J. Garcia & M. Zea (Eds.), Psychological interventions and research with Latino populations (pp. 1–14). Needham Heights, MA: Allyn & Bacon.

Garcia Coll C., Lamberty G., Jenkins R., McAdoo H. P., Crnic K., Wasik B. H., & Vasquez-Garcia H. (1996). An integrative model for the study of developmental competencies in minority children. *Child Development, 67*(5), 1891–1914.

Garcia Coll, C., & Magnuson, K. (1997). The psychological experience of immigration: A developmental perspective. In A. Booth, A. C. Crouter, & N. Landale (Eds.), Immigration and the family: Research and policy on U.S. immigrants (pp. 91–131). Mahwah, NJ: Erlbaum.

Garcia Coll, C., & Szalacha, L. A. (2004). The multiple contexts of middle childhood. The Future of Children, 14(2), 81–97.

Gil, A. G., Vega, W. A., & Dimas, J. M. (1994). Acculturative stress and personal adjustment among Hispanic adolescent boys. Journal of Community Psychology, 22, 43–54.

Gonzales, N. A., Deardorff, J., Formoso, D., Barr, A., & Barrera, M. Jr. (2006). Family mediators of the relation between acculturation and adolescent mental health. Family Relations, 55, 318–330.

Gonsalves, C. J. (1992). Psychosocial stages of the refugee process: A model for therapeutic interventions. Professional Psychology: Research and Practice, 23, 382–389.

Greenberg, M., & Rahmanou, H. (2004). Looking to the future: A commentary on children of immigrant families. The Future of Children, 14 (2), 139–145.

Guarnaccia, P. J., & Lopez, S. (1998).The mental health and adjustment of immigrant and refugee children. Child and Adolescent Psychiatric Clinics of North America, 7, 537–553.

Haboush, K. (2007). Working with Arab American families: Culturally competent practice for school psychologists. Psychology in the Schools, 44(2), 183–198.

Hernandez, D. J. (2004). Demographic change and the life circumstances of immigrant families. The Future of Children, 14 (2), 42–43.

Hones, D. F., & Cha, C. S. (1999). *Educating new Americans: immigrant lives and learning.* Mahwah, NJ: Lawrence Erlbaum Associates.

Hovey, J. D., & King, C. A. (1996). Acculturative stress, depression, and suicidal ideation among immigrant and second-generation Latino adolescents. Journal of American Child and Adolescent Psychiatry 35, 1183–1192.

Huyck, E. E., & Fields, R. (1981). Impact of resettlement on refugee children. International Migration Review, 15 (1/2), 246–254.

Jaycox, L. H., Stein, B. D., Kataoka, S. H., Wong, M., Fink, A., Escudero, P., et al. (2002). Violence exposure, posttraumatic stress disorder, and depressive symptoms among recent immigrant school children. Journal of the American Academy of Child and Adolescent Psychiatry, 41, 1104–1110.

Kaufmann, K. M., & Lay, J. C. (2004). Four commentaries: Looking into the future: Commentary 3. The Future of Children, 14(2), 150–154.

Kao, G. (1999). Psychological well-being and educational achievement among immigrant youth. In D. J. Hernandez (Ed.), Children of Immigrants: Health,

Adjustment, and Public Assistance (pp. 410–477). Washington DC: National Academy Press.

Keller, S. L. (1975). *Uprooting and social change: The role of refugees in development.* Delhi: Manohar Book Service.

Kochar, R., Suro, R., & Tafoya, S. (2005). *The new Latino South: The context and consequences of rapid population growth.* Washington, DC: Pew Hispanic Center.

Kunz, E. (1972). The refugee in flight: Kinetic models and forms of displacement. International Migration Review, 7, 125–149.

Laosa, L. M. (1990). Psychosocial stress, coping and development of Hispanic immigrant children. In F. C. Serafica, A. I. Schuebel, R. K. Russel, P. D. Isaac, & L. Myers (Eds.), Mental health of ethnic minorities (pp. 42–65). New York: Praeger.

Lau, A., Jernewall, N., Zane, N., & Myers, H. (2002). Correlates of suicidal behaviors among Asian American outpatient youths. Cultural Diversity and Ethnic Minority Psychology, 8, 199–213.

Lau, A. S., McCabe, K. M., Yeh, M., Garland, A. F., Wood, P. A., & Hough, R. L. (2005). The acculturation gap-distress hypothesis among high-risk Mexican American families. Journal of Family Psychology, 19, 367–375.

Lee, R. M., Choe, J., Kim, G., & Ngo, V. (2000). Construction of the Asian American Family Conflicts Scale. Journal of Counseling Psychology, 47(2), 211–222.

Mayadas, N., & Segal, U. (2000). Refugees in the 1990s: A U.S. perspective. In P. Balgopal (Ed.), Social work practice with immigrants and refugees (pp. 198–227). New York: Columbia University Press.

McLoyd, V. C. (1998). Socioeconomic disadvantage and child development. American Psychologist, 53, 185–204.

Mushi, S. L. P. (2002). Acquisition of multiple languages among children of immigrant families: Parents' role in the home-school language pendulum. Early Child Development and Care, 172, 517–530.

Nahari, S., Martines, D., & Marquez, G. (2007). Consulting with culturally and linguistically diverse parents. In G. B. Esquivel, E. C. Lopez., & S. Nahari (Eds.). Handbook of multicultural school psychology: An interdisciplinary perspective (pp. 265–289). New York: Routledge (Francis Taylor).

Nightingale, D. S., & Fix, M. (2004). Economic and Labor Market Trends. In M. K. Shields (Ed.), Children of immigrant families. The Future of Children, 14(2), 139–145.

Oades-Sese, G., & Esquivel, G. B. (2006). Resilience among at-risk Hispanic American preschool children. Annals New York Academy of Science 1094(1), 335–339.

Office of Immigration Statistics (2008).Yearbook of immigration statistics 2008. Retrieved January 8, 2009, from http://www.dhs.gov/ximgtn/statistics/publication/yearbooks/shtm.

Ogbu, J. J. (1982). Origins of human competence: A cultural-ecological perspective. Child Development, 52, 413–429.

Peal, E., & Lambert, W. (1962). The relation of bilingualism to intelligence. Psychological Monographs, 76(27), 1–23.

Perez, F. G. (2001). Growing up in Cuban Miami: Immigration, the enclave and new generations. In R. G. Rumbaut & A. Portes (Eds.), Ethnicities: Children of immigrants in America (pp.91–125). Berkeley: University of California Press.

Portes, A., & Rumbaut, R. G. (2001). *Legacies: The story of the immigrant second generation.* Berkeley, CA: University of California Press.

President's Advisory Commission on Educational Excellence for Hispanic Americans. (2003). *From risk to opportunity: Fulfilling the educational needs of Hispanic Americans in the 21st century.* Retrieved May 31, 2003, from http://yesican.gov

Pyke, K. (2005). "Generational Deserters" and "Black Sheep": Acculturative differences among siblings in Asian immigrant families. Journal of Family Issues, 26(4), 491–517.

Rumbaut, R. G., & Portes, A. (2001). Ethnicities: Children of immigrants in America. Berkeley, CA: University of California Press/Sage.

Santiago-Rivera, A. (1995). Developing a culturally sensitive treatment modality for bilingual Spanish-speaking clients: Incorporating language and culture in counseling. Journal of Counseling & Development, 74(1), 12–18.

Silverstein, M., & Chen, X. (1999). The impact of acculturation in Mexican American families on the quality of adult grandchild-grandparent relationships. Journal of Marriage and Family, 61(1), 188–198.

Snyder, C. S., May, J. D., Zulcic, N. N., & Gabbard, W. J. (2005). Social work with Bosnian Muslim refugee children and families: A review of the literature. Child Welfare Journal, 84(5), 607–630.

Suarez-Orozco, C., & Suarez-Orozco, M. (2001). *Children of immigration.* Cambridge, MA: Harvard University Press.

Suárez-Orozco, C., & Todorova, I. (2003). The social world of immigrant youth. In C. Suárez-Orozco & I. Todorova (Eds.), New Directions for Youth Development: Theory, Practice, and Research. Understanding the social world of immigrant youth (pp. 15–24). San Francisco: Jossey-Bass.

Szapocznik, J., Santisteban, D., Kurtines, W. M., Perez-Vidal, A., & Hervis, O. E. (1984). Bicultural Effectiveness Training (BET): A treatment intervention for enhancing intercultural adjustment. *Hispanic Journal of Behavioral Sciences 6(4),* 317–344.

Terizini-Hollar. M. (2008). *Daily hassles, coping, and acculturation as predictors of psychological well-being among Korean-American adolescents.* Unpublished Dissertation. Fordham University.

Tong, V., Huang, C., & McIntyre, T. (2006). Promoting a positive cross-cultural identity: Reaching immigrant students. Reclaiming Children & Youth, 14(4), 203–208.

Tse, L. (1995) Language brokering among Latino adolescents: Prevalence, attitudes, and school performance. Hispanic Journal of Behavioral Sciences, 17, 180–193.

Umana-Taylor, A. J. (2003). Language brokering as a stressor for immigrant children and their families. In M. Coleman & L. Ganong (Eds.), Points & counter points: Controversial relationship and family issues in the 21st century (pp. 157–159). Los Angeles: Roxbury.

United Nations Higher Commission for Refugees (2008). *Global trends: Refugees, asylum-seekers, returnees, internally displaced and stateless persons.* Retrieved July 4, 2009, from http://www.unhcr.org/4a375c426.html.

U.S. Committee for Refugees and Immigrants (2008). *World refugee survey.* Retrieved July 4, 2009, from http://www.refugee.org/about%20refugees.aspx.

U.S. Census Bureau News (2009).*U.S. Hispanic population surpasses 45 million: Population estimates.* Retrieved on July 8, 2009, from http://www.census.gov/PressRelease/www/releases/archives/populatio/013733.html.

U.S. Department of Homeland Security. (2004). *Yearbook of immigration statistics: 2004.* Washington, DC: Author.

Valenzuela, A. (1999). Gender roles and settlement activities among children and their immigrant families. American Behavioral Scientist, 42(4), 720–742.

Vega, W. A., Khoury, E. L., Zimmerman, R. S., Gil, A. G., & Warheit, G. J. (1995). Cultural conflicts and problem behaviors of Latino adolescents in home and school environments. Journal of Community Psychology, 23, 167–179.

Verdugo, R. R. & Flores, B. (2007). English-Language Learners Key Issues. Education and Urban Society, 3(2), 167–193.

Weisskirch, R. S. (2005). The relationship of language brokering to ethnic identity for Latino early adolescents. Hispanic Journal of Behavioral Sciences, 27(3), 286–299.

Weisskirch, R. S. (2006). Changes in perceptions of adolescents and of adolescence from course instruction. College Student Journal, 40(2), 393–399.

Williams, C. L., & Berry, J. W. (1991). Primary prevention of acculturative stress among refugees: Application of psychological theory and practice. American Psychologist, 46, 632–641.

Wong, S. L. (2001). Depression level in inner-city Asian American adolescents: The contributions of cultural orientation and interpersonal relationship. Human Behavior in the Social Environment, 3, 49–64.

Yao, E. (1985). Adjustment needs of Asian immigrant children. Elementary School Guidance and Counseling, 19, 222–227.

Yazbeck-Haddad, Y., & Esposito, J. L. (2000). *Muslims on the Americanization path?* New York: Oxford University Press.

Ying, Y., & Chao, C. (1996). Intergenerational relationship in Iu Mien American families. Amerasia Journal, 22, 47–64.

Ying, Y., & Han, M. (2007). The longitudinal effect of intergenerational gap in acculturation on conflict and mental health in southeast Asian American adolescents. American Journal of Orthopsychiatry, 77, 61–66.

Zapata, J. T. (1995). Counseling Hispanic Children and Youth. In C.C. Lee (Ed). (1995). Counseling for diversity: A guide for school counselors and related professionals. (pp. 85–108). Needham Heights, MA, US: Allyn & Bacon.

Zhou, M., & Bankston, C. L. (1998). *Growing up American: How Vietnamese Children Adapt to Life in the United States.* New York, NY: Russell Sage Foundation.

Zhou, M. (2001). Straddling Different Worlds: The Acculturation of Vietnamese Refugee Children in San Diego. In R. G. Rumbaut & A. Portes (Eds.), Ethnicities: Coming of Age in Immigrant America (pp.187–227). Berkeley and New York: University of California Press and Russell Sage Foundation Press.

Chapter Two

A Culturally Sensitive
Stress-Resilience Model

STRESS AND RESILIENCE

While stress in immigrant children can result in mental health problems, there are a number of individual strengths, support systems, and external resources that if enhanced can serve as protective factors against stress and facilitate the development of resilience. *Resilience* refers to a dynamic process of positive adaptation in spite of exposure to stress and adversity or assaults on the developmental process (Luthar, Cicchetti, & Becker, 2000).

PROTECTIVE FACTORS

Gonzales and colleagues (2004) emphasize two important factors of Hispanic and other minority cultures that may be protective to mental health: (a) *familism* which is identification with and loyalty to nuclear and extended family as support system, and (b) biculturalism which involves the integration of the host and native cultures. Both are protective factors that ameliorate negative outcomes resulting in adolescent well-being. Espousing a strengths-based perspective will include those factors that could better explain the effects of acculturation on families. Valdes (2003) proposed the development of skills in language brokering as a form of giftedness. The skills to understand the culture, meaning, and nuances of language require a degree of sophistication. Orellana et al. (2003) posited that immigrant children are accessing resources on behalf of their families, which is a form of resilience and resourcefulness neglected in research. Therefore, language brokering offers an avenue for strength building in children of immigrants. Regardless of acculturation differences between parent-child or sibling-sibling, successful acculturation to the mainstream culture

17

optimally result in "biculturalism". Biculturalism refers to accommodation without assimilation-acculturation strategy (Gibson, 2001). Bicultural competence results in positive self esteem, social flexibility, and inter-generational cultural transmission (Padilla, 2006). Furthermore, successful transition toward the mainstream culture is characterized by the development of a secure "cross-cultural identity" that optimally balances the values and beliefs of the home and school cultures (Trumbull, Rothstein-Fisch, Greenfield, & Quiroz, 2001).

CULTURAL COMPETENCIES IN THE DEVELOPMENT OF INTERVENTIONS

Cultural competencies involve knowledge and understanding of cultural heritage, values, and behaviors, along with the recognition that levels of acculturation affect delivery of interventions (Al-Krenawi & Graham, 2000). Cultural groups should be differentiated and attention given to the importance of nationality, migration history, and within-group cultural variability when examining acculturative effects (Lau et al., 2005). The processes of *enculturation* and *acculturation* are important to consider when examining the influence of culture on family processes and child outcomes. Researchers contend that these two processes are equally important and operate together to predict adolescent adjustment (Gonzales et al., 2004). Pasch et al. (2006) highlight the importance of the dual processes of acculturation and enculturation among Mexican American families. Helping family members retain those traditional values that may be protective of family functioning, such as familismo and respeto, may better prevent poor outcomes among Mexican American adolescents. At the same time, parents may need to be guided to develop flexibility in understanding the host cultural values to which their children are exposed.

Coping styles, stigma, and mistrust may act as barriers to mental health service use for immigrant populations and help explain limited use of these services (Cauce *et al.*, 2002; Vega *et al.*, 1999). Ho, Yeh, McCabe, and Hough (2007) found that acculturation, as a way of measuring adherence to culture-specific attitudes, values, beliefs, and/or behaviors, is significantly related to disparities in the current mental health care system. Specific parental cultural variables (e.g., the impact of stigma, mistrust, coping styles, or loss of face) should be examined in addition to acculturation. For example, narrative projective techniques reflect how cultures define psychological health. On the Robert's Apperception Test, Egyptian children produced significantly more stories scored for Reliance on Others (Barbopoulos, Fisharah, Clark, & El-Khatib, 2002) which is consistent with a collectivist society. Thus, the ability to gauge and measure acculturation levels is an important competence (Collier, Brice, & Oades-Sese, 2007).

Table 2.1.   Risk and Protective Factors of Immigrant Children and Adolescents

DOMAINS	RISK FACTORS or STRESSORS	PROTECTIVE or RESILIENCE FACTORS
Migration	Trauma	
	Culture Shock	Psychological Adaptation
	Adjustment Disorder	
	Anxiety	
Poverty	Physical/Health Problems	Physical Well-Being
	Cognitive Problems	Cognitive Strategies
		Creativity
		Cognitive Flexibility
Social-Emotional	Social and Behavioral Problems	Self-Esteem
Development	(e.g., gang activity)	Emotion Regulation
	Depression	Spirituality
	Low Self-Esteem	Conflict Resolution
	Substance Abuse	Coping Strategies
Language	Poor Language Skills	Bilingualism
	Selective Mutism	
Academic	Underachievement	Achievement Motivation
	Drop-out	Self-Efficacy
Acculturation	Marginalization	Biculturalism
	Generational Conflict	Ethnic Identity
		Familism

Overall, it is necessary to have cultural sensitivity and awareness of one's own cultural preferences and biases, knowledge of differences and commonalities in cultural values and expressions, and expertise in the process of developing interventions with children and families of culturally diverse background (Ponterotto, Mendelsohn, & Belizaire, 2003). It is also important to research the literature in adopting-adapting evidence based approaches and evaluating the effectiveness of culturally sensitive interventions that facilitate the enhancement of strengths, while addressing stressors that place immigrant and CLD children at risk. A culturally sensitive risk-resilience model (see Table 2.1) provides the basis for developing intervention goals to reduce or ameliorate areas of risk and to enhance or build on areas of strength.

REFERENCES

Al-Krenawi, A., & Graham, J. R. (2000). Culturally sensitive social work practice with Arab clients in mental health settings. Health & Social Work, 25(1), 9–22.

Barbopoulos, A., Fisharah, F., Clark, J. M., & El-Khatib, A. (2002). Comparison of Egyptian and Canadian children on a picture apperception test. Cultural Diversity and Ethnic Minority Psychology, 8(4), 395–403.

Cauce, A. M., Domenech-Rodriguez, M., Paradise, M., Cochran, B. N., Shea, J. M., Srebnik, D., & Baydar, N. (2002). Cultural and contextual influences in mental health help seeking: A focus on ethnic minority youth. Journal of Consulting and Clinical Psychology, 70(1), 44–55.

Collier, C., Brice, A., & Oades-Sese, G. V. (2007). Assessment of acculturation. In G.B. Esquivel, E.C., Lopez, & S. Nahari (Eds.), Handbook of multicultural school psychology: An interdisciplinary perspective (pp. 353–380). New York: Routledge.

Gibson, M. A. (2001). Immigrant adaptation and patterns of acculturation. Human Development (44), 19–23.

Gonzales, N. A., Knight, G. P., Birman, D., & Sirolli, A. A. (2004). Acculturation and enculturation among Latin youth. In K. I. Maton, C. Schellenbach, B. J. Leadbeater, & A. L. Solarz (Eds), Investing in children, youth, families, and communities: Strengths-based research and policy. (pp. 285–302). Washington, DC: American Psychological Association.

Ho, J., Yeh, M., McCabe, K., & Hough, R. L. (2007). Parental cultural affiliation and youth mental health service use. Journal of Youth and Adolescence, 36(4), 529–542.

Lau, A. S., McCabe, K. M., Yeh, M., Garland, A. F., Wood, P. A., & Hough, R. L. (2005).The acculturation gap-distress hypothesis among high-risk Mexican American families. Journal of Family Psychology, 19, 367–375.

Luthar, S. S., Cicchetti, D., & Becker, B. (2000). The construct of resilience: A critical evaluation and guidelines for future work. Child Development, 71(3), 543–562.

Orellana, M. F., Reynolds, J., Dorner, L., & Meza, M. (2003). In other words: Translating or "para-phrasing" as a family literacy practice in immigrant households. The Reading Research Quarterly, 38 (1), 12–34.

Padilla, A. M. (2006). Bicultural social development. Hispanic Journal of Behavioral Sciences, 28, 467–497.

Pasch, L. A., Deardorff, J., Tschann, J. M., Flores, E., Penilla, C., & Pantoja, P. (2006). Acculturation, parent-adolescent conflict, and adolescent adjustment in Mexican American families. Family Process, 45(1), 75–86.

Ponterotto, J. G., Medelsohn, J., & Belizire, L. (2003). Assessing teacher multicultural competence: Self report instruments, observer report evaluations, and a portfolio assessment. In D. B. Pope-Davis, H. L. K. Coleman, W. M. Liu, & R. L. Toporek, Handbook of multicultural competencies in counseling & psychology (pp. 191–210). Thousand Oaks, CA: Sage.

Trumbull, E., Rothstein-Fish, C., Greenfield, P. M., & Quiroz, B. (2001). Bridging cultures between home and school: A guide for teachers. Mahwah, NJ: Lawrence Erlbaum Associates.

Valdes, G. (2003). *Expanding definitions of giftedness: The case of young interpreters from immigrant communities.* Mahwah, NJ: Lawrence Erlbaum Associates.

Vega, W. A., Kolody, B., Aguilar-Gaxiola, S., & Catalano, R. (1999). Gaps in service utilization by Mexican Americans with mental health problems. American Journal of Psychiatry, 156(6), 928–934.

Chapter Three

Theoretical Bases of Narrative Therapy

NARRATIVE THERAPY

Narrative therapy is an intervention that lends itself to the development of resilience in immigrant and culturally diverse children in coping with stress and in the attainment of psychological adaptation, creativity, literacy-linguistic skills, social emotional growth, self esteem, and motivation. There are different forms of narrative therapy (e.g., journaling, bibliotherapy, storytelling, autobiography) but essentially it is a strength-based approach. Its aim is to provide a non-judgmental environment and a safe therapeutic relationship in which the client(s) (i.e. children) can develop a greater sense of awareness and mastery over stressful life events through the use of narratives. Narrative therapy is consistent with a culturally responsive approach based on the premises of individual, social, and cultural constructivist theories (Esquivel & Flanagan, 2007).

NARRATIVE THEORY

The term "narratives" is used as a metaphor for thought processes that interact with cognitive, memory, linguistic, affective, and perceptual functions in enabling the individual and social group to interactively construct and share the meaning of experiences (Crossley, 2003). Reality does not exist in itself or outside of this 'meaning-making' process but is rather the embodiment of personal and social interpretations of everyday events and the history of life experiences. This process of interpretation is described by Bruner (1986) as a propositional way of knowing that is storytelling-like in nature and differs from paradigmatic, logical or rational thinking. The personal nature of this process is based on personal constructivism which posits that individuals impose structure on the temporal flow of experiences and interpret these according to past constructs for understanding the meaning of events (Sarbin, 1986; Gerrig, 2005).

In turn, social constructivism represents the view that the individual and the social group interactively share and expand the meaning of experiences through personal (self expression), oral and written traditions, and various storytelling modalities (e.g., biographies, anecdotal records, journals). Cultural constructivism refers to the role of the larger group in interpreting and transmitting cultural values and historical experiences from one generation to the next. Culture is viewed as the result of the collective construction of historical reality through narratives and narrative processes. Meaning is created through shared interactions, negotiations, communication, and intersubjective understanding among individuals in a culture (Hoshmand, 2000; Howard, 1991). McAdams (2001) expresses the narrative constructivist view of culture as:

> The stories told at day's end created a shared history of people, linking them in time and event, as actors, tellers, and audience in an unfolding drama of life that was made more in the telling than in the actual events to be told. . .Stories are less about facts and more about meanings. In the subjective and embellished telling the past, the past is constructed-history is made (pp.622-623).

There are narrative variations across cultures along historical dimensions (e.g., past history, experiences of a people), social dimensions (e.g., ways of transmitting culture, child-rearing practices), mental dimensions (values, attitudes, ideas, symbolism, metaphors), and material dimensions (e.g., texts, stories, artifacts) (Brockmeier, 2002).

NARRATIVES AND SOCIAL EMOTIONAL DEVELOPMENT

Narratives are an integral part of social emotional development and mental health. McAdams (1993) formulated a developmental framework to describe the progression of narrative thinking. Young children start to construct stories based on associations to culturally transmitted values in the form of myths, stories, fables, and nursery rhymes. These mediated stories and folk tales help children make sense of early experiences and serve as a basis (in the form of schemas) for assigning meaning to the flow of on-going experiences. Folk tales also allow young children to live out and work through developmental issues in a safe manner (Bettleheim, 1976). School age children process more intentional and goal oriented narratives expressed in the ability to create or relate their own stories. Adolescents develop philosophical schemas for interpreting experiences with a greater sense of temporal perspective (i.e., past, present, future) and are able to reconstruct their own stories or project ideals into the future with a greater sense of personal identity. This integrative ability is reflected in journal writings of that age group. A classical illustration of adolescent narratives is Anne Frank's *The Diary of a Young Girl* (Frank & Pressler, 1995), a moving account of a young girl's personal stories as she made sense of her experiences in the context of the Holocaust. Her personal "stories" portray not only the developmental strivings common to young girls in finding their identity, but also her own search for meaning in the midst of traumatic events in her life and the lives of her people. Anne Frank's entry of Wednesday, April 5, 1944 states:

> I finally realized that I must do my schoolwork to keep from being ignorant to get on in life, to become a journalist, because that's what I want! I know I can write. . .it remains to be seen whether I really have talent. . .I need to have something besides a husband and children to devote myself to!...I want to be useful or bring enjoyment to all people, even those I've never met. I want to go on living even after my death! And that's why I'm so grateful to God for having given me this gift which I can use to develop myself and to express all that's inside me! When I write I can shake off all my cares. My sorrow disappears, my spirits are revived! But, and that's a big question, will I ever be able to write something great, will I ever become a journalist or a writer?...I hope so, oh, I hope so very much because writing allows me to record everything, all my thoughts, ideals, and fantasies (pp.246-247).

NARRATIVES AND STRESS

While the narrative process is a major source of strength in the social emotional development and psychological adjustment of children under normative circumstances, exposure to adverse life situations such as trauma or significant prolonged stress may result in developmental arrests or disruption of narrative functions. Children who are resilient as a result of a combination of individual protective factors and family support systems and resources, interacting over time to provide endurance under adverse circumstances, are able to sustain a meaningful sense of integrity and mastery in coping with stressors. Conversely, children who have limited individual strengths (e.g., cognitive, temperamental) and/or lack sources of family support and resources are prone to experience the negative effects of stress. In terms of the narrative metaphor, there may be disruptions in thought, memory, linguistic, affective, perceptual, and/or integrative functions that affect the meaningful and positive interpretation of life experiences and sense of identity.

Culturally diverse and immigrant children are exposed to stressors of poverty, migration, and acculturation, discontinuity of everyday life experiences, and disrupted temporal sequence of events. These adverse circumstances, along with the possible loss of family members, peers, and sources of support in school and community, place these children at risk of negative developmental and psychological outcomes. It is therefore important from a preventative standpoint to understand and implement interventions that address their needs in a culturally appropriate and effective manner.

NARRATIVE INTERVENTIONS

Narrative interventions are based on the assumption that individuals may be guided to reconstruct their understanding of past experiences, interpret or reinterpret traumatic events, modify faulty assumptions from varied perspectives, adopt more flexible ways to process events, bridge gaps in and integrate their life stories, develop a greater sense of agency as narrators of their own story, and become better able to create future life-enhancing experiences. Essentially narrative interventions may help to build or restore the narrative process. Narrative therapy may be accomplished through individual or group therapeutic modalities or used conjointly with family therapy.

When implementing narrative therapy with children, the process involves allowing the child to express feelings, heal from past trauma, symbolically externalize conflicts, vicariously identify with characters, or role play solutions and alternative outcomes through the use of narrative techniques. The aim is for the child to learn with the guidance of a therapist and in shared interaction with peers to develop a sense of self esteem and mastery in making sense of experiences and ultimately finding meaning in life (Gardner, 1971).

When using narrative interventions, it is also important to consider individual, developmental, and socio-cultural factors. For example, the use of narrative therapy with young children may be embedded within a play therapy context and/or combined with puppetry and drawing techniques. More specifically, culturally sensitive narrative interventions should incorporate critical aspects of culture (e.g., cultural history, social values, family systems-extended family, acculturation level, language and processing styles, culture-specific stories and materials or multicultural texts), while addressing developmental and cultural adjustment concerns.

REFERENCES

Bettleheim, B. (1976). *The uses of enchantment: The meaning and importance of fairy tales.* New York: Random House.

Brockmeier, J. (2002). Introduction: Searching for cultural memory. Culture and Psychology, 8, 5–14.

Bruner, J. (1986). *Actual minds, possible worlds.* London: Harvard University Press.

Crossley, M. (2003). Formulating narrative psychology: The limitations of contemporary social constructionism. Narrative Inquiry, 13(2), 287–300.

Esquivel, G. B., & Flanagan, R. (2007). Narrative methods of personality assessment in school psychology. Psychology in the Schools, 44, 271–280.

Frank, O. H., & Pressler, M. (Eds.) (1995). *The diary of a young girl: Anne Frank.* New York: Doubleday.

Gardner, R. A. (1971). *Therapeutic communication with children: The mutual storytelling technique.* Riverdale, NJ: Jason Aronson.

Gerrig, R. J. (2005). Moral judgments in narrative contexts. *Behavioral and Brain Sciences, 28,* 550.

Hoshmand, L. T. (2000). Narrative psychology. In A. E. Kazdin (Ed), Encyclopedia of psychology (vol. 5, pp. 382–387). Washington, DC: American Psychological Association.

Howard, G. S. (1991). Culture tales: A narrative approach to thinking, cross-cultural psychology, and psychotherapy. American Psychologist, 46(3), 187–197.

McAdams, D. P. (1993). *The stories we live by: Personal myths and the making of the self.* New York: William Morrow & Co.

McAdams, D. P. (2001). *The person: An integrated introduction to personality psychology (3rd ed.).* Fort Worth, TX: Harcourt College.

McAdams, D. P., Orellana, M. F., Reynolds, J., Dorner, L., & Meza, M. (2003). In other words: Translating or "para-phrasing" as a family literacy practice in immigrant households. Reading Research Quarterly, 38(1), 12–34.

Sarbin, T. R. (1986). *Narrative psychology: The storied nature of human conduct.* Westport, CT: Praeger.

Chapter Four

Culturally Sensitive Narrative Interventions

The concept of narratives from a cross-cultural perspective forms the basis for narrative interventions with children and adolescents of immigrant and cultural-linguistically diverse backgrounds. As a basis, it is important to understand how narratives are tied to human social experience, the culture-specific and universal nature of stories, the healing value of cultural narratives combined with other modalities, and the role of culturally sensitive narratives in facilitating adjustment among children and adolescents of immigrant background.

THE ORIGINS OF NARRATIVES: THE SOCIAL GLUE PERSPECTIVE

Dautenhahn (2002) provides an evolutionary explanation for the origins of narratives; one that intrinsically links stories to the evolving socialization process in humans. In a world divided into 7 continents, 200+ countries, and a human population of over 6 billion, one overarching mechanism that functions to create order and cohesiveness within and between culturally distinct, similar and dissimilar societies of all sizes is narrative storytelling.

The history of humankind reveals storytelling has evolved from primate "social grooming" which is a direct physical means of identifying and establishing relationships with members of the same group. Communication then evolved to use language and dialogue; proving to be more efficient with the natural trend for groups and communities which were increasing in size and social complexity (Dunbar 1993). Narrative storytelling, described as the most efficient and natural way to communicate, especially about others (Bruner, 1990, 1991), provides a means to disseminate social knowledge from one generation to the next, and even between geographically separated locations (Donald, 1993). As Franz de Waal aptly stated of primate politics, indentifying friends and allies, predicting behavior of others, knowing how to form alliances, manipulating group members, making war, love and peace, are important social functions (De Waal, 1982). The same holds true for modern human society. The tradition of narrative storytelling when used with children, has a definitive beginning, causative middle and reactionary ultimate end, with didactic intentions toward social bonding and cohesiveness– in essence, it is a "social glue" (Dautenhahn, 2002).

Storytelling in this modern age comes in all forms, from storybooks, epics, radio broadcasts, grandparent nostalgia, to television news broadcasts. These methods have been expanded to incorporate technology through email, chat rooms over the internet, and text messaging. Social networking, or more precisely, "digital social networking," is one of the major avenues that young and old people have been using to share or "blog" or "tweet" the daily occurrences and major life events or accomplishments in the internet. The internet provides access to over millions of people where life stories can be posted instantaneously. Pictures and videos reflecting life stories (e.g., YouTube) expands ones's ability to disseminate social information effectively and efficiently in a matter of milliseconds once you click on the "send" button. A person's digital social network is composed of family, friends, co-workers, prospective clients and employers- expanding to friends of a friend of a friend as well as international acquaintances. Digital social networking currently includes MySpace, Facebook, Twitter, LiveJournal, and Bebo- at this moment. Mass popularity of using these methods are better illustrated by their current statistics as of the month of June 2009 in Quantcast.com- Facebook is used by 91.2 Million while MySpace is used by over 63 million people. What is popular for a particular month changes quickly to another.

UNIVERSAL AND CULTURAL VARIATIONS IN NARRATIVES

Written narratives are predicated on oral and performance traditions (Gates, 1989). Cross-culturally, narratives can be universally characterized through use of symbols, recurring themes (quests), characters, heroes (i.e., romantic, heroic, sacrificial and antagonists /conflict) and story structure and plot types (Hogan, 2003). Universal themes also include good versus evil, and the conflict between the individual and self, another person, family, society, nature, and the cosmos. The basic structural organizations are somewhat consistent across cultures and languages (Mandler, Scribner, Cole, & DeForest, 1980). For example, children who speak, Chinese, English, German, Spanish, Hebrew and Turkish follow similar structures such as characters engaging in actions related to resolving problems or complications (Munoz, Gillam, Pena, & Gulley-Faehnle, 2003). However, differences were found regarding the content of the story - nature of the problem, relationships between characters, and type of narrator explanations- reflecting cultural and linguistic experiences. For example, folklore stems from "action of people and their roots in social and cultural life" (Bauman, 1992, p. 2).

Children learn to use narrative formats valued by their cultural community to recount events. For example, Japanese narratives are elegantly compressed or succinct; resembling haiku poems (Miname & McCabe, 1995). Narratives encountered in U.S. schools are more descriptive in nature elaborating on a single event. Stories are central to learning and instruction in Native Americans and Alaskan native education—fostering attention, imagination, metaphoric thinking, and flexibility and fluency of thought (Rogoff, 2003). Native American narratives are about tricksters, tribal histories, creation, and migration. Themes emphasize:

- Communality
- Humor
- Repetition
- Circularity
- Themes of Natural Elements
- Symbol
- Character
- Time
- Season
- Spiritual Traditions

For African American children, church narratives play a central role in socialization (a process where adults teach children what they need to know to participate in various social activities of a given society)—understanding the meaning of the Scriptures in relation to everyday life. African and African American children follow an oral tradition and enjoy role-playing and using different voices (Goodwin, 1990). Storytelling among Black South Africans center on themes related to tradition and freedom and the conflict between the two groups (Scheub, 1996). Other themes include famine, drought, infestation, innate intelligence and wit, and the supernatural (Okafor, 1983). These themes reflect what is important to a given society or culture.

Classical folk tales from Puerto Rico called "cuentos" center around a character called Juan Bobo, a young boy who is not very smart and gets into all sorts of problems but in the end all works out for the best. These tales emphasize the value of simplicity and the trust in the providential nature of God. Narratives from Mexican Americans originate from oral narratives that recount travels, family, and community. This is in contrast to *event-casting* or telling about an ongoing activity in linear sequence as is more common in U.S. culture (Heath, 1986). Hispanic Americans are less likely to talk about sequence of events unlike European North Americans, Japanese, and African Americans (McCabe, 1997). Stories of Hispanic Americans relate more to family and relationships as well as reactions and evaluations of events (Silva & McCabe, 1996).

NARRATIVES' RELATIONSHIP TO PHYSICAL AND MENTAL HEALTH

Cross-cultural research has found health benefits of writing that go beyond culture and language (Paez, Velasco, & Gonzalez, 1999; Solano, Donati, Pecci, Persichetti, & Colaci, 2003; Yamamoto, Yogo, & Suzuki, 2004). Individuals who wrote about their traumatic experiences demonstrated (Pennebaker & Beall, 1986):

• Improved physical health
• Reduced number of visits to the doctor by 50% after 2 months of writing
• Enhanced immune systems as measured by objective medical tests

Using certain linguistic features of writing stories also predicted improved health (Pennebaker, Mayne, & Francis, 1997). For example, people who used high levels of positive words of emotion (i.e., love, care, happy) rather than negative words of emotions (e.g., sad) demonstrated improved health. Using moderate amounts of negative emotion words as opposed to low or high amounts reduced the number of visits to the doctor. The increasing use of words that refer to causality (i.e., because, reason) and insight (i.e., understand, realize) from the first to last session showed health improvements. In addition, the use of pronouns from each session reflected the changes in perspective in the story. Ramirez-Esparza and Pennebaker (2006) posit that these changes in writing may reflect the patterns of optimism, story construction, and understanding different perspectives in a person's life-story.

In terms of bilingualism, using both native and second language in writing has also been beneficial. When Mexican-American and Korean-American bilinguals wrote about their emotional stories in both languages, both groups exhibited more emotional and health benefits (Kim & Pennebaker, 2006).

NARRATIVES AND LITERACY

Beside its therapeutic benefits, narratives build academic skills that facilitate literacy and reading skills. Researchers have found that cross-culturally, narrative skills can predict literacy and reading comprehension (Cain & Oakhill, 1996; Chang, 2006; Tabors, Snow, & Dickinson, 2001). Oral language skills that are de-contextualized serve as a precursor to reading (Snow, 1983). Therefore, narratives used as a form of mental health intervention in schools offer children both a therapeutic and academic (literacy) benefit.

Early childhood is a crucial period of development to build oral language skills that build on academic success (Chang, 2006). Therefore, family and school prevention and intervention programs that enhance narrative skills in young children are of value to their social-emotional and academic resilience, as well as builds family relationships through communication.

Although narratives in Spanish and in English were found to be identical among bilingual children in Southeastern Texas (McCabe & Bliss, 2003), some differences exist in terms of content. Young children were more likely to include initiating events and attempts to solve problems in Spanish, while older children were likely to include more consequences in English (Fiestas & Pena, 2004). These differences may reflect a bicultural difference in narrative style, culture-specific differences, or differences of exposure to certain stories at home versus school.

NARRATIVE THERAPY AND DRAWINGS

Use of drawings can facilitate young children's ability to talk about emotional experiences and facilitate narrative expression. Drawings in combination with narratives provide insights to inner experiences of children related to traumatic experiences such as displacement due to war, living through a natural disaster, or planned relocations. Because the environment plays a central part in a child's life related to identity, emotion regulation, and sense of well-being (Manzo, 2003), displacement leaves the child feeling disoriented and confused.

Igoa (1995) provides an excellent practical application of drawings and narratives based on children's creation of a filmstrip story, such as "The Little Egg" written by Dung, a 10½ year old Vietnamese girl:

> One day in a little town of America, there was an egg sitting in a nest on a branch of a tree. It just sat there all winter, all spring, all summer, and all fall. When the next year came, it still sat there all winter again. In the spring, it

hatched into a beautiful bird. It started to run around the tree. Soon, it began to fly farther away from the nest. It flew and it flew and it flew to Vietnam. It landed on a window of a house. . .that belonged to a little girl. The little girl's name was Tai-Hing. In the morning she looked out the window and saw a tired-out little bird. She picked it up slowly and gently and brought it to her room. She cared for it, fed it, and kept it warm. The bird began flying all around the house. The bird grew bigger and bigger. . .and soon it was time to let it go. She put it on the open window and the bird flew away. Soon, the bird found a mate, and they made a big nest. The two birds came to visit Tai-Hing every year. She was expecting them every year. The End. (pp. 64-66)

Igoa reflects that Dung's story illustrated the immigrant child's need for "nesting" during the initial stages of acculturation. The two years of incubation represented the two years when she was silent and unable to communicate with anyone at school; the egg was alone in the nest. Dung reflected ". . . the little egg that was me at M. P. Brown [school]. It was terrible. I was a little egg and the whole world was around me . . . I was in the shelter, and it cracked. I didn't know what to do". Dung later reflected on her story when she was older that it illustrated the need for a safe and nurturing environment to adjust and develop. She stated:

Vietnam was my heritage and I wanted to keep it. Someday I hope to return for a visit. The first year in America, the time just lagged. No one could understand me. I had a terrible time. I couldn't communicate with anyone. I couldn't even tell my parents my problem because they were adapting too. I was that little egg, and the whole world was around me. I was in a shelter, for I was lost and afraid. I was also insecure. I developed an insecurity complex because I couldn't do things by myself. The egg cracked open one day and turned into a beautiful bird. That was my hope, my wish. That everything would turn out okay someday. I was afraid that I was not going to make it then. The bird flew to Tai-Hing, who represented the person I wished I had to help me grow up and adapt to American society. With the problem of insecurity, I needed someone to care for me, to hold my hand and say, "It's all right, I'll help you. Don't be afraid." I needed someone to set me on the right track. I needed her caring so I could be stronger. I just needed her caring so that I could begin to do things on my own. So that is why Tai-Hing let the bird go when the bird got bigger. I believed that all stories should have a happy ending, getting married and staying happy (p. 97).

Use of drawings (Gross & Hayne, 1998) can:

- increase that amount of information children report
- reduce perceived demands during a clinical interview
- enhance retrieval of memories

- organize narratives to tell a better story
- provide distance between children and their problem

To illustrate the above benefits, adolescents who had experienced Hurricane Katrina were more likely to share their traumatic stories when drawings were used (Looman, 2006). In relation to migration, drawings in combination with narratives facilitated the healing process of "balseritos" or "rafters," Cuban refugee children who were traveling in the treacherous waters to the U.S. (de Valle, McEachern, & Sabina, 1999). Utilization of drawings in combination with writing activities also produced positive outcomes for these children, as measured by their academic grades, classroom behavior, attendance, and teacher feedback after the first marking period. Therefore, it appears that illustrating and writing about emotional experiences, have a cathartic effect in relieving traumatic experiences opening the door to more positive outcomes, allowing children to move forward and concentrate on school and other developmentally appropriate tasks. As children mature, narratives evolve from simple folktales to complex stories relying less on visual representations.

Uses of narratives have also been found to help refugee and asylum-seeking children cope with their ordeal (Kohli, 2006). Beek and Schofield (2004) refer to these children as "closed book" children. Kohli states:

> These children present as compliant, polite yet troubled individuals who worry about safely talking to others, having been instructed by their families of origin not to reveal facts, feelings and thoughts to those who are caring for them. However, little is known about why and the ways in which silence, secrets and the types of 'truths' they tell about themselves both help and hinder their search for resettlement (p. 708).

The 'silence' that characterizes these children's narratives reflects their fear about sharing their experiences as well as wiping away memories (Melzak, 1992). These children suffer from losses, family members left behind, and have let go of any hopes of a reunion. Silence, however, has been reported to represent both vulnerability and resilience (Papadopoulos, 2002). The assumption is that children are purposely silent to allow healing to take place, hiding and managing pain. So, silence serves as a protective factor rather than an indicator of psychopathology. Drawings may be used as an effective medium to slowly work through the "silence" and find its way to healing and the open expression of feelings.

Among similar interpretations, White (1997) differentiates narratives as 'thick' versus 'thin' stories. Thick stories tap complex underlying trauma and distress whereas thin stories are simpler superficial ways of expressing these feelings. The role of the clinician is to tease out the thick stories trapped within thin stories (Kohli, 2006) and drawings help facilitate this process.

Another form of therapeutic intervention combining drawings with storytelling is Narrative Exposure Therapy, which has been adapted to be used with children six years old and older. Narrative Exposure Therapy with children (KIDNET) uses a rope or string to represent a lifeline and flowers and rocks are placed on the lifeline to signify positive and negative events, respectively. Drawings and role-playing are also incorporated in the therapy. For example, four to six sessions of KIDNET has been found to reduce post-traumatic stress disorder (PTSD) and depressive symptoms with Somali refugee children (ages twelve- to fourteen-years-old) at the 9-month follow-up session (Onyut et al., 2005). KIDNET emphasizes an integration of emotional and sensory memory within a life story.

NARRATIVES AND PUPPETS

Use of puppets has been widely documented to be effective in a variety of clinical applications and interventions. For example, puppets have helped hospitalized children cope with illness and separation from parents (Woltmann, 1940) and have also helped abused or traumatized children feel more comfortable playing out their experiences than interacting directly with a therapist, similar to the spontaneous way they use family dolls or action figures (Carter 1987; Seinfeld, 1989). Children identify with puppets and project their feelings onto the puppets; allowing children to depersonalize their feelings and share them indirectly with the therapist.

Puppets that reflect or represent cultural values and traditions have been shown to be more effective for culturally linguistically diverse children. For example, given that Native Americans value storytelling and humor, clown-like figures are often found in their folklore. Use of animal puppets during storytelling has been also found to be effective with Native American children (Herring & Meggert, 1994). The authors have found multicultural puppets that represent different cultural and ethnic groups can be very effective in teaching children about feelings, emotional literacy, conflict resolution, and pro-social skills. The authors have also found puppets "of color" useful in training teachers how to teach children conflict resolution skills in their classrooms.

In terms of diversity or multicultural education, puppets have also been used to teach children about acceptance and tolerance of differences. The "Kids on the Block" puppet program (Aiello, 1988) is an example of a culturally sensitive approach that teaches nondisabled children to understand and appreciate those who are different. Puppets can also represent a variety of conditions, disabilities, or situations such as cerebral palsy, mental retardation, epilepsy, diabetes, child abuse, teenage pregnancy, and divorce.

BIBLIONARRATIVE THERAPY: UNITING ORAL AND WRITTEN LIFE-STORIES

Biblionarrative therapy is a technique that uses both telling and writing about important life events with children (Eppler & Carolan, 2005). The therapist or clinician starts out by interviewing the child about key elements of the child's life story by asking open-ended questions, such as, what are your earliest memories of your family? These questions provide details and context of the child's life. The therapist then asks the child to write his or her life story by providing prompts. For example, Eppler and Carolan suggest the following prompts that can be used with grieving children:

(a) "Before my mom/dad died . . . " (Family or individual before the problem),
(b) "When I found out my mom/dad died . . ." (During the "problem" saturated story),
(c) "Now that I think/feel about my mom/dad. . ."
(d) "In the future I think. . ."

Eppler and colleagues state that if a child gets stuck, the therapist can use prompts such as "what happened next?" or "who else was involved?" Use of metaphors (comparisons of how two dissimilar things are alike) help externalize the problem such as "The Raincloud" that passed over our house to signify the sadness of a parent death.

Biblionarrative is flexible in its application and can be conducted in one or several sessions. The therapist uses the information in the biblionarrative as well as the same words to join the child in reconstructing his or her life story. Eventually, children can create their own stories and become authors of their own self-made books. Although this narrative technique is appropriate for children ages nine years or older because children at this age have the ability to reflect on their experiences and can acknowledge thoughts and feelings, it may also be adapted to young children from culturally and linguistically diverse backgrounds. Initially, the therapist can start by conducting bibliotherapy, using books that illustrate and talk about young children's experiences such as coming to a new country, first experiences of going to a new school, missing family left behind in another country, not knowing how to speak the language of a new country, feelings of isolation, and acculturating to a new place. Examples of these books include *My Name is Yoon* by Helen Recorvits, *The Name Jar* by Yangsook Choi, *Tar Beach* by Faith Riggild, and *Mi Sueno de America* by Yuliana Gallegos. Through shared reading, the therapist can prompt children by asking them about their own experiences. The therapist can help a younger child write down his or her life story by using simple words and pictographs. Therefore, this creative technique can be used to facilitate adjustment and acculturation of young immigrant preschool children. Reconstructing or repairing life stories at an earlier age may help in fostering resilience among these children, especially if their migration experience was traumatic. Helping children understand these experiences will help with their adjustment and emotional well-being. When ready, children may then be able to share their life stories and narrative experiences in a small group situation.

NARRATIVES AS A CULTURALLY-SENSITIVE TECHNIQUE

In essence, culture is composed of a collection of stories from a particular society and therefore has great influence in people's lives. From the *Our Creative Diversity: The UN World Commission on Culture and Development Report,* culture is describes as ". . . the whole complex of distinctive spiritual, material, intellectual and emotional features that characterizes a society or a group. It includes creative expressions, community practices and material or built forms." Culturally-sensitive therapy refers to a technique that is designed to take into consideration cultural factors such as values, traditions, language, attitude, laws, and implicit theories (general expectations or beliefs of a culture not stated) and adapting interventions to reflect them.

A culturally sensitive narrative technique with Hispanic children and adolescents (ages nine- to thirteen-years-old), has been found to be effective for treatment of conduct disorder, anxiety, and phobia (Costantino, Malgady, & Rogler, 1994). This method uses the TEMAS (Tell-Me-A-Story) comprised of pictures with family scenes, neighborhoods, and multiracial families- usually impoverished, inner-city communities. Similarly, Cuento Therapy uses "cuentos" or folktales with Hispanic children to help change maladaptive behaviors and deal with acculturation stress. Cuentos conveys a message or moral that uses characters to motivate and model beliefs, values, and behaviors. Mother and child dyads engage in reading and talking about these folktales (Costantino et al., 1986). Themes in folklore have been found to be correlated with what is valued in a culture such as parenting practices, emphasis in achievement, and strides for independence (McClelland & Friedman, 1952).

In comparison to other types of therapy, cuentos therapy was found to be more effective than art/play therapy and control groups in reducing anxiety and building coping skills of bilingual immigrant children (Kindergarten to Grade 3). Cuentos therapy also increased social comprehension relative to control and art/play therapy groups. Cuentos was adapted for use with Hispanic adolescents in the form of biographies of cultural heroes with similar positive outcomes.

A culturally-sensitive technique that has been implemented with adolescents and older individuals is the use of Dichos or proverbs—a saying that reveals truth or folk wisdom. Zuniga (1991) states:

> Each cultural group uses their proverbs to express their perspective on situations, problems, dilemmas, or the paradox of the human condition. . .
> [used as] guidelines in the development of attitudes, moral values, and social behaviors . . . reveal[ing] a worldview or psychology of a people (p. 480).

Examples of dichos are "Del Viejo el consejo" (experience gives advice), Haz bien y no mires a quien" (charity is its own reward), and "Dime con quien andas y te dire quien eres" (tell me who your friends are and I will tell you who you are). Proverbs similar in content can also span cross-culturally. For example, the following is a proverb that refers to the importance of solidarity: *"Pita uko," si kuenda. Kwenda ndi "Tiyende kuno!"mbwa inzifu yemanya* (Mozambique), or *"Vai nesta direcção" não é andar. Andar significa "vamos embora juntos!"* (Portuguese) means *"Go in that direction" does not mean that you go. To go means, "Let's go together!"* These truths are often transmitted to children and adolescents by adults from generation to generation. It is important in the therapeutic setting to distinguish between maladaptive behaviors and those behaviors that are misjudged as inappropriate due to differences in cultural values.

Another narrative-holistic approach uses spirituality and has been demonstrated to be effective among culturally diverse adolescents who display poor adjustment to foster care (Kirven, 2000). This method uses Myers' Theory of Optimalization, which builds on an optimal worldview and a holistic way of thinking based on interpersonal relationships with family and the community. This method uses five steps called Holistic Integration Techniques to build a spiritual affiliation with a Higher Power by helping clients confront adversity and turn them into positive outcomes despite current circumstances. These five steps are (see Kirven, 2000 for further details):

• Using hardships as measures to build positive outcomes
• Accepting limitations and capabilities
• Building a spiritual consciousness

- Using the environment as a classroom to teach self and others
- Establishing a collective empowerment way of thinking (building a supportive network)

In sum, narratives have evolved as "social glue" that binds humanity together whether in the form of picking off fleas from an aunt's primate back (i.e., social grooming) to sitting in front of a computer "blogging or tweeting" family and friends, locally or internationally, depending on one's digital social network. Universally, oral and written narratives reflect themes such as bravery, perseverance, romance, heroism, and good versus evil. Variation in style, format, and expression, however, reflects what a given society or culture values and nurtures. In addition to the functional role of communication, linguistic features (i.e., use of emotional words) of narratives are beneficial to physical and mental health as well as education (i.e., literacy). Consequently, narratives offer an effective mode of intervention in the schools, especially when used in combination with drawings, bibliotherapy, and puppets.

When narrative therapy is adapted to reflect cultural values, traditions, languages, and attitudes, it can be an effective culturally-sensitive technique for children of diverse backgrounds. Narratives can help immigrant children heal and develop strengths in the process. In essence it is in the sharing of and listening to the diverse stories that the unique voices of silenced children can emerge, bringing new meaning to their life story.

REFERENCES

Aiello, B. (1988). The kids on the block and attitude change: A 10–year perspective. In H. Yuker (Ed), Attitudes toward persons with disabilities. (pp. 223–229). New York: Springer.

Bauman, R. (1992). *Story, performance, and event: Contextual studies of oral narrative.* New York: Cambridge University Press.

Beek, M., & Schofield, G. (2004). Promoting security and managing risk: contact in long-term foster care. In E. Neil & D. Howe (Eds.), Contact in adoption and permanent foster care: Research, theory and practice (pp. 124–143). London: BAAF.

Bruner, J. (1990). *Acts of meaning.* Cambridge, MA: Harvard University Press.

Bruner, J. S. (1991). Nature and uses of immaturity. In M. Woodhead, R. Carr, & P. Light (Eds.), Becoming a person. (pp. 247–275). Florence, KY: Taylor & Frances/Routledge.

Cain, K., & Oakhill, J. (1996). The nature of the relationship between comprehension skill and the ability to tell a story. British Journal of Developmental Psychology, 14, 187–201.

Carter, S. R. (1987). Use of puppets to treat traumatic grief: A case study. Elementary School Guidance & Counseling, 21(3), 210–215.

Chang, C. (2006). Linking early narrative skill to later language and reading ability in Mandarin-speaking children. Narrative Inquiry, 16, 275–293.

Costantino, G., Malgady, R. G., & Rogler, L. H. (1986). Cuento therapy: A culturally sensitive modality for Puerto Rican children. Journal of Consulting at Clinical Psychology, 54, 639–645.

Costantino, G., Malgady, R. G., & Rogler, L. H. (1994). Storytelling through pictures: Culturally sensitive psychotherapy for Hispanic children and adolescents. Journal of Clinical Child Psychology, 23, 13–20.

Dautenhahn, K. (2002). The origins of narratives: In search of the transactional format of narratives in humans and other social animals. International Journal of Cognition and Technology, 1, 97–123.

de Valle, P., McEachern, A. G., & Sabina, M. Q. (1999). Using drawings and writings in a group counseling experience with Cuban rafter children, "Los Balseritos." *Guidance and Counseling, 14*, 20–28.

de Waal, F. (1982). *Chimpanzee politics: Power and sex among apes.* London: Jonathan Cape.

Donald, M. (1993). Precis of Origins of the modern mind: Three stages of the evolution of culture and cognition. Behavioral and Brain Sciences, 16, 737–791.

Dunbar, R. I. M. (1993). Coevolution of neocortical size, group size and language in humans. Behavioral and Brain Sciences, 16, 681–735.

Eppler, C., & Carolan, M. T. (2005). Biblionarrative: A narrative technique uniting oral and written life-stories. Journal of Family Psychotherapy, 16, 31–43.

Fiestas, C. E., & Pena, E. D. (2004). Narrative discourse in bilingual children: Language and task effects. Language, Speech, and Hearing Services in Schools, 35, 155–168.

Gates, H. L. (1989). Introduction. In L. Goss & M. E. Barnes (Eds.), Talk that talk: An anthology of African American storytelling (pp. 15–19). New York: Simon & Schuster.

Goodwin, M. H. (1990). *He-said-she-said: Talk as social organization among Black children.* Bloomington, IN: Indiana University Press.

Gross, J., & Hayne, H. (1998). Drawing facilitates children's verbal reports of emotionally laden events. Journal of Experimental Psychology, 4(2), 163–179.

Halliday, M. A. K. (1979). The development of texture in child language. In T. Myers (Ed.), *The development of conversation in discourse.* Edinburgh: Edinburgh University Press.

Heath, S. B. (1986). Taking a cross-cultural look at narratives. Topics in Language Disorders, 7(1), 84–94.

Herring, R. D., & Meggert, S. S. (1994). The use of humor as a counselor strategy with Native American Indian children. Elementary School Guidance & Counseling, 29(1), 67–76.

Hogan, P. C. (2003). *The mind and its stories: Narrative universals and human emotion.* Cambridge: Cambridge University Press.

Igoa, C. (1995). *The inner world of the immigrant child.* New York: St. Martin's Press.

Kim, Y., & Pennebaker, J. W. (2006). Exploring language, social behavior and health, Manuscript under review. University of Texas at Austin.

Kirven, J. (2000). Building on strengths of minority adolescents in foster care: A narrative-holistic approach. Child & Youth Care Forum, 29, 247–263.

Kohli, R. K. S. (2006). The sound of silence: Listening to what unaccompanied asylum-seeking children say and do not say. British Journal of Social Work, 36, 707–721.

Looman, W. S. (2006). A developmental approach to understanding drawings and narratives from children displaced by Hurricane Katrina. Journal of Pediatric Health Care, 20, 158–166.

Mandler, J. M., Scribner, S., Cole, M., & DeForest, M. (1980). Cross-cultural invariance in story recall. Child Development, 51, 19–26.

Manzo, L. C. (2003). Beyond house and haven: Toward a revisioning of emotional relationships with places. Journal of Environmental Psychology, 23(1), 47–61.

McCabe, A. (1997). Developmental and cross-cultural aspects of children's narration. In M. Bamberg (Ed.), *Narrative development: Six approaches* (pp. 133–174). Mahwah, NJ: Lawrence Erlbaum Associates.

McCabe, A., & Bliss, L. S. (2003). *Patterns of narrative discourse.* Boston: Pearson Education.

McClelland, D. C., & Friedman, G. A. (1952). A cross-cultural study of the relationship between child-training practices and achievement motivation appearing in folk tales. In G. E. Swanson, T. M. Newcomb, & E. L. Hartley (Eds.), *Readings in Social Psychology.* New York: Holt.

Melzak, S. (1992). Secrecy, privacy, repressive regimes and growing up. Bulletin of he Anna Freud Centre, 15, 205–224.

Miname, M., & McCabe, A. (1995). Rice balls and bear hunts: Japanese and North American family narrative patterns. Journal of Child Language, 22(2), 423–445.

Munoz, M. L., Gillam, R. B., Pena, E. D., & Gulley-Faehnle, A. (2003).Measures of language development in fictional narratives of Latino children. Language, Speech, and Hearing Services in Schools, 34, 332–342.

Okafor, C. A. (1983). *The banished child: A study in Tonga oral literature.* London, UK: Folklore Society.

Okafor, C. A. (1997). Overcoming obstacles: Academic achievement as a response to racism and discrimination. Journal of Negro Education, 66, 83–93.

Onyut, L. P., Neuner, F., Schauer, E., Ertl, V., Odenwald, M., Schauer, M., & Elbert, T. (2005). Narrative exposure therapy as a treatment for child war survivors with posttraumatic stress disorder: Two case reports and a pilot study in an African settlement. BMC Psychiatry, 5, 1–9.

Paez, D., Velasco, C., & Gonzalez, J. S. (1999). Expressive writing and the role of alexythimia as a dispositional deficit in self-disclosure and psychological health. Journal of Personality and Social Psychology, 77(3), 630–641.

Papadopoulos, R. K. (2002). *Therapeutic Care for Refugees. No Place Like Home.* London: Karnac.

Pennebaker, J. W., & Beall, S. K. (1986). Confronting a traumatic event: Toward an understanding of inhibition and disease. Journal of Abnormal Psychology, 95(3), 274–281.

Pennebaker, J. W., Mayne, T. J., & Francis, M. E. (1997). Linguistic predictors of adaptive bereavement. Journal of Personality and Social Psychology, 72(4), 863–871.

Ramirez-Esparza, N., & Pennebaker, J. W. (2006). Do good stories produce good health? Exploring words, language, and culture. Narrative Inquiry, 16, 211–219.

Rogoff, B. (2003). *The cultural nature of human development.* New York: Oxford University Press.

Scheub, H. (1996). *The tongue is fire: South African storytellers and Apartheid.* Madison, WI: University of Wisconsin Press.

Seinfeld, J. (1989). Therapy with a severely abused child: An object relations perspective. Clinical Social Work Journal, 17(1), 40–49.

Silva, M. J., & McCabe, A. (1996). Vignettes of the continuous and family ties: Some Latino American traditions. In A. McCabe (Ed.), *Chameleon readers: Teaching children to appreciate all kinds of good stories* (pp. 116–136). New York: McGraw-Hill.

Snow, C. E. (1983). Literacy and language: Relationship during the preschool years. Harvard Educational Review, 53, 15–189.

Solano, L., Donati, V., Pecci, F., Persichetti, S., & Colaci, A. (2003). Postoperative course after papilloma resection: Effects of written disclosure of the experience in subjects with different alexithymia levels. Psychosomatic Medicine. 65(3), 477–484.

Tabors, P. O., Snow, C. E., & Dickinson, D. K. (2001). Homes and schools together: Supporting language and literacy development. In D. K. Dickinson & P. O. Tabors (Eds.), Beginning literacy with language (pp. 313–334). Baltimore, MD: Paul H. Brookes.

White, R. A. (1997). Dissociation, narrative, and exceptional human experiences. In S. Krippner & S. M. Powers (Eds), Broken images, broken selves: Dissociative narratives in clinical practice. (pp. 88–121). Philadelphia, PA: Brunner/Mazel.

Winslade, J., & Monk, G. (1999). *Narrative counseling in schools: Powerful and brief.* Thousand Oaks, CA: Corwin Press.

Woltmann, A. G. (1940). The use of puppets in understanding children. *Mental Hygiene, 24,* 445–458.

Yamamoto, K., Yogo, M., & Suzuki, N. (2004). Intra and interpersonal factors inhibiting the disclosure of emotional episodes. *The Japanese Journal of Research on Emotions, 11,* 73–81.

Zuniga, M. E. (1991). "Dichos" as metaphorical tools for resistant Latino clients. Psychotherapy: Theory, Research, Practice, Training, 28(3), 480–483.

Chapter Five

Multicultural Narratives and Puppetry: Educational Applications

This supplemental chapter provides a discussion of applied professional experiences related from the voice of the author (Jarvis) on the implementation of culturally sensitive narratives combined with the use of puppetry and offers practical vignettes of educational, diagnostic, and therapeutic value for children of cultural and linguistically diverse backgrounds.

CULTURALLY SENSITIVE NARRATIVE LITERATURE

Years of experience teaching culturally diverse students has revealed a scarcity of relevant children's literature available to English Language Learners (ELLs) and culturally diverse students in the U.S. schools. A search for existing children's literature evidenced a distinct lack of engaging stories and familiar characters to serve as identity models for children of cultural diversity.

The scarcity of multicultural literary resources is in striking contrast with the need for young and emerging readers (especially those from diverse cultures) to relate to the setting and characters in the stories they are reading in a way that enhances their ability to derive meaning from the text. Classroom observations suggest that children are more easily engaged when they can choose a book to read in which they can find themselves in a personal and culturally meaningful way (Feger, 2006; Richard-Amato & Snow, 1992). The general lack of interesting stories and relatable literature for children of color or cultural diversity has made literacy instruction and therapeutic interventions for multicultural students an intriguing challenge.

Recently, a number of multicultural and bilingual books for children have emerged (see reference list on Appendix C). Moreover, public domain stories, fairy tales, and folk tales have been adapted and retold for diverse populations of young readers. Stories such as "Goldilocks and the Three Bears" or "Ricitos de Oro y Los Tres Osos" in Spanish are available from several publishers in Easy-to-Read trade books for young readers. Resources for translating a favorite story or fairy tale into another language are available on the Internet as well (see Appendix C).

Even more significant is finding the same story or theme in literature written in the language of a child's country of origin, and as a variation in the second language. Resources and lists of good children's literature in their native languages can be found on the Internet (see Appendix C). As children become more familiar with the same story in their second language, they begin to identify similar characters, events, storylines, vocabulary, phrases, and certainly an underlying message. These connections define the "AHA!" moment, and can contribute a first real positive step, and personal triumph, in the acquisition of a second language and the development of self-awareness helpful in the acculturation process.

PUPPETRY AS CULTURALLY SENSITIVE ART FORM

What is a puppet? One definition: A puppet is a figure, inanimate object, or animate object (fingers), whose movements can be controlled by someone using hand movements, strings, or rods. Puppets can even be full-body figures, in which the puppeteer inside uses arms and legs in imaginative ways to make the puppet character come alive, for example, Big Bird on Sesame Street (Copp, 2004).

Puppets have been part of human history from earliest times, as storytellers, entertainers, educators, and a means of self-expression. Some of the earliest puppets were tribal ritual masks with hinged jaws or jointed skulls, used in religious ceremonies. Eventually, puppets evolved from these masks to doll-like figures with moving limbs.

Puppetry, as an art form, may have originated in China, where shadow puppets were used to tell stories. These shadow puppets were rod puppets made of animal skin used to cast shadows to be viewed by the audience. Turkish puppeteers created three-dimensional figures that were the first, simple, articulated puppets, constructed to bend at the waist as well as arms and legs, emulating more natural human movement. Native American Indians used puppets in their corn festivals and ceremonial dances. Ancient Egyptians made jointed puppets from terra cotta, the same material that is used to make flowerpots. Ancient Greeks, such as Plato and Aristotle, mention Puppet Theater in their writings as well (Copp).

However, the real credit for the survival of puppetry goes to those traveling puppeteers who kept the art and craft of puppetry alive over the centuries. Traveling troupes of entertainers, such as jesters, jugglers, puppeteers, and storytellers, were the keepers of history and folklore from cultures around the world through oral tradition. Just as a puppeteer breathes life into each figure, so did nomadic puppeteers breathe new life into tales, myths, stories, and even history (Copp).

During the Middle Ages the Church used puppets to spread church doctrine and teach liturgical practices to a population that could neither read nor write. During the fourteenth and fifteenth centuries, puppetry became more popular with the working class. Street performances and fairs were the most common places to enjoy puppetry in outdoor theater settings. In the sixteenth century, character hand puppets with expressive molded heads and cloth bodies were most popular. In Europe, "Punch and Judy", featured in outdoor theatre shows, became popular traveling show figures. Since politics was a favorite topic, "Punch and Judy" could express controversial political opinions without exposure to the same punitive consequences as their human counterparts (Copp).

In the United States, the evolution of puppetry includes "Stars" such as "Howdy Doody" (marionette), "Kukla, Fran, and Ollie" (hand puppets), "Topo Gigio" (Italian foam-rubber rod puppet, whose name translates as "Louis Mouse"), "Johnny" creation of Señor Wences (a face drawn on a hand, propped up by a headless doll, by Spanish ventriloquist Wenceslau Moreno, better known as "Señor Wences"), Mr. Rogers and his "Royal Family" of puppets, "Jerry Mahoney" (ventriloquist Paul Winchell), "Charlie McCarthy" (ventriloquist Edgar Bergen), "Lamb Chop and Charlie Horse" (ventriloquist Shari Lewis). Most recently, the "Muppets" (rod and full-body puppets created by Jim Henson), became popular characters used to teach concepts, language, and much more in both English and Spanish. Many of these "Stars" continue to entertain and educate, as important members of the family tree of puppetry.

Historically, humankind has been intensely occupied with storytelling, as evidenced by our own multi-cultural and international practice of oral tradition; namely, passing stories from generation to generation before the written word. People used storytelling to define the world around them, explain natural events, and perhaps even try to control those events. It is not difficult to imagine our ancestors, trying to share or explain a concept, using hand motions or signals, and/or inanimate objects (rudimentary puppets), to communicate, illustrate a concept, or make a point.

Telling stories, expressing our thoughts, creating and even controlling other worlds, as we define our own, has always been part of our evolutionary process. A puppet, as an extension of one's self, can be an anonymous creature or person, and in some cultures even a god, used to explore, embrace, explain, or even critique. Historically, puppetry is a relatively safe venue for self-expression without consequence.

MULTICULTURAL PUPPETRY AND NARRATIVES

Multicultural puppets may be combined with narratives as a culturally sensitive modality. An illustration of an adapted version of "Goldilocks and the Three Bears" presented at the end of this chapter as "Curlylocks and the Brooklyn Bears" has been written in English, rewritten, and adapted by the author in collaboration with children of Latino, Hispanic, Chicano, and South American background, (among others), specifically to be performed with puppets. These puppets and scripts allow children of immigrant background to enjoy a possibly familiar story, relate to the characters (Goldilocks is Curlylocks), and to play a role, remaining anonymous, thereby creating a comfortable venue for self-expression.

In search for stories and themes that would appeal to multicultural students and support acculturation, educators, psychologists, and consultants working with ELL students typically seek out books about children in cultures from every continent, and beyond. Specific research included stories about the author's own students who were from Russia, France, Italy, Cuba, The Dominican Republic, Mexico, Peru, Central America, India, Vietnam, and Australia . . . among others.

NARRATIVES AND PUPPETRY
AND SECOND LANGUAGE DEVELOPMENT

During the process of second language acquisition (after the first language is established), children progress through four distinct stages as they learn a second language in a new setting (Tabors & Snow, 2001). The first stage is characterized by a child's attempts to communicate in his or her native language. When children realize that they do not understand, and are not being understood, they move rapidly to the second phase. This next stage may be fraught with frustration over the inability to communicate. At this point the child may enter the non-verbal stage or silent period and not talk at all, while still processing language in a covert manner. To a teacher, this behavior may be interpreted as non-compliance, or cause a teacher to suggest the need for testing and special services. The third stage is the first stage of rudimentary verbal communication. After much practice, and data gathering, the ELL child begins to communicate using short phrases, and words that he or she has memorized in a particular context. The final stage is a more comfortable place from which children develop productive expressive language. This stage is characterized by coupling those successful phrases and ideas from the third stage, with words from an expanding vocabulary (Tabors & Snow, 1994).

Stories, songs, folk tales, and fairy tales, provide the context in which children can successfully build expressive language skills. Puppetry and Storytelling not only provide the context, but a venue in which a child in any of the previously mentioned stages of language acquisition, may participate and learn. Observing the excitement as children make connections between cultures, as they recognize and find themselves in stories, is quite gratifying and can enhance self esteem and motivation to learn the second language and acculturate to the host culture without losing a sense of their own ethnic identity (Krashen, 1982).

The more connections that can be made between a child's native language and the second language, the more likely the child can make the anticipated adjustment. One approach, often cited as a "best practice", is to teach math, science, and social science in a child's native language. Acquisition of the second language, English in this case, would be part of a separate Language Arts Curriculum. Content is taught in the child's native language, in conjunction with instruction in the intricacies of learning, speaking, reading, and writing English. "Additive Bilingualism"—mastering the native language while gaining proficiency in English—has shown to have cognitive and social-emotional advantages (Oades-Sese & Esquivel, 2006).

The second language process may be facilitated using narratives and puppetry. Puppetry is a simple way to act out personal feelings, explore, explain, communicate ideas, entertain, and educate. This mediated narrative experience may have particlar value for a child who has not mastered the tools for expressive language in his or her native tongue or a second language.

The "Curlylocks" script (Appendix A) is illustrative of a culturally sensitive narrative combined with puppetry to help facilitate communication skills for ELL and bilingual children. This adapted version is characterized by "code switching" or flexibility in incorporating vocabulary from two languages without losing the sense of language structure and meaning (Kecskes, 2006). Likewise, the underlying theme of the story is maintained while borrowing from diverse cultural elements and dimensions. This script has been modified in various languages and performed by many groups of children, (i.e., ELL, Special Needs, and General Classroom) in several states. The children have an opportunity to memorize the scripts, rehearse until ready to perform, and then perform a story for their peers in a way that facilitates language development and vocabulary acquisition. These opportunities are an intrinsic result of the performance process. Before the children are ready to "Take the Show on the Road", they must know their parts, the staging directions, be in the right place at the right time, and deliver their lines accurately, with expression.

Teaching a skill or concept is one of the best ways to own it yourself. These young actors, after the first (or second), performance, invite the audience to participate in brief vignettes with the original puppets from the performance, closely supervised and coached by the puppeteers. These young puppeteers have taken complete ownership, and have exhibited great pride in their abilities, accomplishments, and performances. They are thrilled to share their new knowledge, language abilities, and acting and puppetry skills with their peers.

Next, members of the audience are offered the opportunity to create their own versions of the featured characters, from finger puppets and stick puppets, to marionettes. There are countless stories, with universal messages for diverse populations that could be adapted to present images and characters with whom young English Language Learners can relate.

Puppetry and storytelling may also be used in classroom settings to develop language and literacy skills in the context of second language learning strategies. In June of 2007, the U.S. Department of Health & Human Services, through the Administration for Children and Families, suggested a list of "Ten Things You Can Do to Support English Language Learners."

- *Consider English language learners when addressing the class.* Use Language and concepts that are inclusive and which are easily understood by all students in your group.
- *Give frequent feedback.* Acknowledge efforts, accomplishments and struggles. Model the language you would like to hear. Let children know that you are following their progress.
- Watch children before you engage them. *Sit quietly and observe what children are doing, encourage their efforts and step in to thoughtfully support additional learning.*
- *Bring language to silent moments.* Guide children's learning by asking questions and talking about what children are doing. When teachers ask questions that challenge children's thinking, they are guiding their learning.
- *Help children to think out loud.* Describe what you see children doing and help them to think about their work. Having children think out loud offers you insight into how they are learning.
- *Talk with children to help them put their actions and ideas into words.* Doing this helps children be clear about what they are doing and strengthens what they are learning.

- *Ask children open-ended questions.* Questioning children not only extends their learning but it also lets you see their learning and progress. Open-ended questions, on the other hand, ask a child to give more than a one- or two-word answer and have many possible right answers.
- *Create situations for children to talk with their peers.* Children can teach each other and learn a lot from one another. Children can sometimes learn more from a peer buddy than from an adult or teacher.
- *Use props that children can see and feel with stories and songs.* Children understand better when they can use more than one sense . . . when they can hear, see, touch, smell and feel rather than just hear. This works well for children whose first language is not English.
- *Create a language-rich classroom.* Using labels in many languages, signs, books, charts, and media, make sure there are many opportunities for children to find words in the classroom.

Incorporating culturally sensitive narratives, puppetry, role playing, and other creative materials and media with language learning strategies may be implemented with minimal effort in any classroom. Using a multi-modality approach works well for all students but is particularly of value for children whose first language is not English.

VIGNETTES

The following anecdotes are from the author's own personal experiences, thus the change in "voice" from third to first person. These vignette excerpts are based on personal-professional experiences implementing narrative and puppetry "best-practice" techniques of educational and therapeutic value.

NARRATIVES AND PUPPETRY: A PERSONAL STORY

Childhood experiences leave lasting impressions on every individual. At the age of six, while my father was on sabbatical in Thailand, this author remembers working with my mother at the School for the Deaf in Bangkok. We made simple hand, stick, and finger puppets, and acted out indigenous and classic stories with her Thai students. This experience was my first exposure to puppets as a fun and educational venue for communication and storytelling.

Upon our family's return to the United States, our collection of puppets had grown substantially. Many of those puppets have survived for more than

50 years, and are still used as models for young puppeteers, as they construct their own puppets and write their own stories.

VIGNETTES ON THE USE OF
NARRATIVES AND PUPPETRY IN THE CLASSROOM

Publishers of children's literature have discovered the attraction that puppets have for children. Puppets often are offered and sold to accompany a particular book or story, as a package deal, to help the characters come alive. Even simple stick puppets created from illustrations in a book can create a more tangible means of communication and promote learning in the classroom.

Puppetry can be a very simple activity. The teacher might read a selection of books to the class and then ask the children to choose a favorite. Once the children have selected their story, they are invited to draw the characters on cardboard or card stock and cut them out. (We created black and white drawings of characters in the story, on card stock, that the children could color and decorate, then staple to craft sticks to be used as stick puppets.) The children are then asked to retell and reenact the story from the book with the puppets they have made. These puppets can take the form of stick puppets, finger puppets, or shadow puppets

In our educational practice, we selected and supplied age-appropriate examples of children's literature from which each group of children could choose. Scripts were written, printed, modified, and rewritten to create stories chosen by the students, who then created puppets for production. Roles in scripts were color-coded to make it easier for students to identify their own characters. Stage notes and other information were color-coded as well. Scripts were recorded on tape for rehearsals, so that performers could hear the nuances, vocabulary, and inflection appropriate to each character. Classroom teachers and special educators helped students create sets, props, and backdrops for each performance (See resources in Appendix B).

The fledgling puppeteers not only had to memorize a script, know all their entrances and exits, but also had to know the flow of the story. Inside the puppet theater were color-coded notes for each child's cues and order of appearance of each of the characters. Our puppeteers took great pride in a successful performance. They all worked as a team to support each other, and be worthy of the applause at the end of a performance. After the final scene, the stage manager would gather the puppeteers in front of the stage with their puppets. The children were asked to introduce themselves, their puppets, and then take a bow. The boost in self-esteem was clearly written on the face of each puppeteer.

VIGNETTES ON NARRATIVES AND PUPPETRY AS A TOOL FOR LITERACY AND DUAL LANGUAGE DEVELOPMENT

As special educators at a rural school in Northern Vermont we used puppetry as an incentive for children with special learning needs who had given up on the whole process of reading. As far as they were concerned, learning to read might never happen for them. However, our previous success with puppets inspired a new incentive program for our non-readers, and with the support of the reading specialist, director of special services, and school principal, the implementation of our new program began.

Every Friday (provided they finished their schoolwork on time and were doing their personal best), children could declare the day "Puppet Friday". Each age group could choose two stories to read and think about, and then vote on their favorite one. Students in kindergarten through fourth grade had six weeks to complete their puppet projects.

After extensive research about reaching and teaching ELL students, and the success of puppetry in the above reading and language acquisition program, we adopted the same approach with our ELL students from Italy, Russia, Cuba, and Vietnam. The children were encouraged to bring in books from home (many in their native language) that they could share with the class. The children did "picture walks" and then with parental input, pieced together the story and engaged in 'shared reading experiences' with their parents. Recognizing and teaching to various learning styles meant that our students could use all of their senses to make the most out of learning using all available resources.

Our older students used classroom computers to type out the story (with assistance), and then could invent, dictate, or write dialog for the characters to make them come alive. A large, non-serif font, compatible with what we used in our reading program, was selected for use at each grade level. Our young puppeteers loved to ad-lib, tell jokes and add humor that varied with each performance. Really relevant ad-libs and jokes were included in our written scripts! It was a real "Badge-of-Honor" for a child to have a joke or ad-lib added to an existing script. To really understand a language, it is very telling to see that children can recognize humor and idioms in their second language. Adding humor (e.g., bilingual puns) and dialogue was a strong indication that the ELL students "got it!"

We discovered early on, that creating audiotape recordings for rehearsal helped with differences in pronunciation, grammar, and syntax that the puppeteers absorbed as they perfected their roles. In addition, hardcopy scripts were color-coded for each character. As our techniques evolved and became increasingly user-friendly, it was easier for our ELL students to acquire their second language in a more natural way, similar to the ways in which they had learned their first languages.

Over the years, we developed a Repertory Puppet Company, and each new class looked forward to taking their shows "On the Road" throughout the school year. We designed mobile theaters that could be moved from classroom to classroom. Our Repertory Company was even invited to perform at the local Children's Library three years in a row. Some of our puppeteers were students with special needs as well as ELL students. Parents and other teachers participated in this process with the children and helped design and construct puppets, sets, and new mobile theaters on wheels as our numbers increased. The development of literacy skills and language acquisition was the demonstrable goal for these children. As predicted, our students made rapid and remarkable progress in reading and bilingual skills, as well as self-esteem.

School-aged children are particularly vulnerable to the challenges of coordinating two cultures, potentially creating psychological and behavior problems (Berry, 2005). Teaching in a local bilingual school setting was a key factor in this author's expanding interest in helping children of immigrant background adjust to their new circumstances. This particular school had several types of classroom structure. Older children were grouped in classroom where Spanish was spoken for Science, Social Studies, Math, and Language Arts. English was taught as a second language, and the goal by the end of the year, was to help students make the transition to a bilingual classroom in which the predominant language was English.

Younger children were grouped in classes in which teaching was conducted in English, and Spanish was spoken at home. When working with a small group, Spanish-speaking puppets were used to teach content and Spanish. The puppets could only speak Spanish, and so the children had to respond in Spanish. During Language Arts, the teacher would only speak English, teach in English, and the children would be compelled to respond in English. This approach turned out to be an effective way to use both languages, and enhance language acquisition in both languages.

The immigrant families worked very hard to be successful in their new country. Often the students, as young as second grade, would rush home from school to take care of younger siblings while parents left for second, and even third jobs, necessary for the survival of the family. These young, school-age children became their family's link to their new environment. The children not only were learning English in school, but also acted as "language brokers" or, translators, interpreters, negotiators, and tutors for their parents and extended family members (Valenzuela, 1999), many of whom might never master a second language. While these responsibilities were stressful for the students, they were able to turn a challenging situation into a positive source of resilience.

VIGNETTES ILLUSTRATING THE USE OF
NARRATIVES AND PUPPETS AS THERAPEUTIC TOOLS

One of the best techniques to get children to talk about themselves and their life issues is to provide a surrogate character through which they can communicate thoughts and feelings too difficult to discuss with another person. In collaboration with mental health professionals at a local hospital, this author worked with children of immigrant families in counseling. We helped these children to communicate difficult issues and experiences as new immigrants, using puppets. The young participants in the program created puppets from craft foam balls, fabric scraps, and other craft materials, and then used them to communicate and act out scenarios that were of concern for the children.

Sometimes the experiences were fun, and we played, and acted out stories. At other times the sessions were painful, and sometimes even turned into enactments of repressed anger. A particularly poignant example is that of one child who spent two weeks constructing a puppet that represented an adult member of his family. This child spent a great amount of time creating this puppet, and making sure that its features were authentic. Upon successful completion of the puppet, to the author's surprise, this child smashed and destroyed his creation. It was later discovered that there had been a history of child abuse in his family.

While working at a teaching hospital in Vermont, our hospital auxiliary created simple Teddy Bears of washable materials to help the children who were coming into the Emergency Department, and to help young patients and family members to have the most positive experience possible. The city of Burlington was home to a diverse population from many countries, including a large Vietnamese population, as well as Sudanese, Russian, Latino, and Hispanic immigrants. As a step further, our Emergency Department bears were transformed into puppets to be used to demonstrate hospital procedures. Along with their young human counterparts, the bear puppets were evaluated, treated, and even bandaged. Upon leaving the hospital, the children were given the puppets to take home. The same puppets often returned to the hospital, or Emergency Department, on subsequent visits. Behavioral observations of children served to reflect the positive outcomes of this intervention.

REFERENCES

Berry, J. W. (2005). Acculturation: Living successfully in two cultures. International Journal of Intercultural Relations, 29(6), 97–712

Copp, L. A. (2004). *Brief history of puppetry.* Retrieved August 8, 2009, from http://sunniebunniezz.com/puppetry/puphisto.htm

Feger, M. V. (2006, April). "I want to read": How culturally relevant texts increase student engagement in reading. *Multicultural Education.* San Francisco, CA: Caddo Gap Press.

Kecskes, I. (2006). The dual language model to explain code-switching: A cognitive-pragmatic approach. Intercultural Pragmatics, 3, 257–283.

Krashen, S. D. (1982). *Principles and practices in second language acquisition.* Oxford, England: Pergamon Press.

Oades-Sese, G., & Esquivel, G. B. (2006). Resilience among at-risk Hispanic American preschool children. Annals New York Academy of Science 1094(1), 335–339.

Opie, P, & Opie, I. (1974). *The classic fairy tales.* New York: Oxford University Press.

Phinney, J. S., Romero, I., Nava, M. & Huang, D. (2001). The role of language, parents, and peers in ethnic identity among adolescents in immigrant families. Journal of Youth and Adolescence, 30, 135–153.

Richard-Amato, P. A., & Snow, M. A. (1992). *The multicultural classroom: Readings forcontent-area teachers.* Reading, MA: Addison-Wesley.

Tabors, P., & Snow, C. (1994). English as a second language in preschools. In F. Genesee (Ed.), Educating second language children: The whole child, the whole curriculum, the whole community (pp.103–125). New York: Cambridge University Press.

U.S. Department of Health & Human Services (2007). *Ten things you can do to support* English language learners. Retrieved July 4, 2009, from http://www.acf.hhs.gov/programs/region10/resources/region_10_minutes/handout_10_things_english_lang_learners_call_05_14_2008.html

Valenzuela A. (1999). Subtractive schooling: U.S. Mexican youth and the politics of *caring.* Albany, NY: State University of New York Press.

Appendix A

Sample Script

DISCUSSION OF ADAPTATION OF
"GOLDILOCKS AND THE THREE BEARS"

There are variations from countless cultures of endless fairy tales and folk tales. The story of "Goldilocks and the Three Bears" for example, probably from England, was most likely written in the early nineteenth century. There is some dispute about the birth of the original "Goldilocks and the Three Bears." The story, from oral tradition, actually appeared in a hand-written book in the early 1830s (Opie & Opie, 1974).

Our particular adaptation written for puppets has been performed in schools in Vermont, Maryland, and New Jersey. It was exciting to see children recognize stories with universal themes that they remembered from their countries of origin, and in their native language. It provided an opportunity to expedite vocabulary acquisition, and make the children more comfortable as they learned their parts for each performance.

Puppets, even the simplest stick, paper plate, or paper bag ones can be used very effectively to provide a means of communication, even when there is no common language, and particularly in the absence of spoken language. A child can remain anonymous and still communicate feelings and thoughts through the words and actions of a puppet. Puppet personas are used for clinical application and intervention, therapy, teaching children about feelings, emotional literacy, conflict resolution, pro-social skills, social tolerance, and multicultural differences and similarities. In all the afore-mentioned venues, puppets have proven to be a valuable tool and basic form of communication and acculturation for children of immigrant backgrounds.

SAMPLE SCRIPT USING A
PUBLIC DOMAIN STORY OR FOLK TALE
"CURLYLOCKS AND THE BROOKLYN BEARS"

Narrator:	"This is the story of 'Curlylocks and the Brooklyn Bears'." "HERE is where our story begins, deep in Prospect Park, in the Boro of Brooklyn, in the State of New York, in the United States of America . . ."
Narrator:	"One Saturday morning, Papá Oso, Mamá Osa, and Osita Bebé were sitting in their Prospect Park tree house, planning their weekend."
Osita Bebé:	"It's Saturday Papá, what will we do today?"
Papá Oso:	"Well Niña, I am cooking the chicken for my famous Quesadillas de Pollo, (Chicken and Tortillas), for lunch!"
Osita Bebé:	"M-m-m-m-m . . . Mamá, can we have Flan de Coco for dessert?"
Mamá Osa:	"Oh yes, Niña. Let's walk to the bodega while the chicken is cooking. We'll buy eggs for our flan."
Osita Bebé:	"Papá, the chicken already smells good! Don't forget milk, Mamá."
Mamá Osa:	"And, don't YOU forget to close the door behind you, Niña."
Osita Bebé:	"Si, Mamá."
Narrator:	"So, the Bears left their tree house to walk to the bodega on Fifth Avenue to buy eggs and milk for their dessert." "Uh-oh, Niña forgot to close the kitchen door, again!"
Narrator:	"Now, at the edge of Prospect Park, lived a little girl named Curlylocks. She missed her home in Mexico. She missed playing outside with all her cousins. Her family had moved to New York, and none of the children she had met in her building spoke Spanish. She was very lonely."
Curlylocks:	"I wish I had some new friends. I am very lonely."
Narrator:	"On Saturdays, no-school days, Curlylocks loved to walk through Prospect Park and visit the animals that lived there."
Curlylocks:	"Buenos Dias . . . Bebé Rabbit, Señor Squirrel, and Señorita Raccoon. Yes, it is good to see you too, but I'll walk a little farther today. I might meet some new friends I can talk to."
Narrator:	"Soon, she came to a huge tree with a small door."
Curlylocks:	"A door in a tree . . . that's strange . . . I wonder who would live in a tree with a door!
Narrator:	"The door was ajar, and she could see into the kitchen."
Curlylocks:	"Hello," she called, "Is anyone home?"

Narrator:	"There was NO answer!"
Curlylocks:	"I guess no one is home. M-m-m-m, and what's that smell? It smells delicious. I'm hungry! And look, the door is open."
Narrator:	"Curlylocks tiptoed up to the tree, and carefully peeked around the door."
Curlylocks:	"Well, I don't SEE anyone. I don't think anyone will notice if I have something to eat. I think I'll try just a small bite of that delicious-smelling chicken!
Curlylocks:	"Ouch, it's too hot! But look, there are tortillas on the table. It looks like someone is might be making Quesadillas for lunch. I'll just have a few bites of tortilla as a snack."
Narrator:	"So, Curlylocks sat down and sampled a small bite of the largest tortilla."
Curlylocks:	"OH! This tortilla is too big! I can't get a real bite, just a few crumbs."
Narrator:	"Then Curlylocks decided to try some of the medium-size tortilla."
Curlylocks:	"Oooooooh, this looks good, I'll try a small bite of THIS medium-size tortilla. BUT, this one is still too big I can only take a small bite."
Narrator:	"Just then, Curlylocks noticed one more tortilla."
Curlylocks:	"I'll just take a taste of THIS small tortilla. It's just my size."
Narrator:	"So, she took a tiny bite of the smallest tortilla. And what do you think she said?"
Curlylocks:	"M-m-m-m, I love this little tortilla, it's JUST RIGHT! I am soooo hungry that I'm going to eat it ALL UP!"
Narrator:	"Well, Curlylocks was just as hungry as she thought! She had eaten the WHOLE tortilla."
Curlylocks:	"Ohhhh, but now I'm VERY full; It's time for a quick nap."
Narrator:	"Curlylocks wandered through the den, looking for a comfortable place to take a nap. She climbed the stairs to the second floor. First, she came to a large-size bed."
Curlylocks:	"Oh, this is a nice big bed; I'll just cuddle up under the blanket. Wait a minute, this bed of wood is too hard. I'll try the next one."
Narrator:	"So, Curlylocks hopped into the medium-size soft, soft bed."
Curlylocks:	"This looks nice and soft . . . Oh, no, it's TOO soft, HELP! (The bed swallowed up Curlylocks.)"
Narrator:	"Curlylocks struggled and struggled, and finally climbed out of that bed."

Curlylocks:	"Whew! That bed tried to swallow me UP. Oh look, there's ONE more small-size bed, [YAWN] I'm really tired, I think I'll just lie down for one little minute . . . Oooooh, I LOVE this little bed. It's JUST RIGHT. ZZZZZZZZZZZZZZZ"
Narrator:	"Well, Osita Bebé's small bed WAS just right. And what do you think Curlylocks DID? Yes, she fell asleep, thinking of delicious quesadillas for lunch, and dreaming about how GOOD dessert and an ice-cold glass of milk would taste after her nap."
Narrator:	"Shhhhhh . . . if you listen carefully, you can hear footsteps. The Bears are almost home . . ."
Papá Oso:	"It's NICE to be home. Now I'm really hungry for lunch. It smells like our chicken is ready to eat."
Osita Bebé	"I am tired . . . that was very long walk, and now I'm HUNGRY!"
Mamá Osa:	"I'm hungry too, and we were lucky to buy Flan at the store. I won't have to make it from scratch."
Narrator:	"Suddenly, Papa Bear stopped short in front of their tree, Mama bumped into him, and Baby bumped into Mama. Mama leaned out to look past Papa."
Mamá Osa:	"Uh-oh, Niña, you forgot to close the kitchen door and it is wide open. I hope everything is OK."
Papá Oso:	"Better let me go first . . . Mira! . . . Someone has been chewing on my tortilla! Here, look at the teeth marks!"
Mamá Osa:	"You're right, AND someone has taken a whole bite out of MY tortilla!"
Osita Bebé	"Ay, Si Si! Someone has been eating MY tortilla, too! And guess what?"
Narrator:	"Yes, Curlylocks had eaten Baby Bear's tortilla ALL UP! WELL, the Bears were VERY curious to find out who had eaten their tortillas. You see, Papá Bear was a famous chef at the Bogotá Latin Bistro, in Park Slope, Brooklyn. People came from everywhere to eat the food at his restaurant."
Papá Oso:	"Maybe we should search the rest of our home to be sure that whoever ate our lunch is gone . . . You know that I don't like surprises! Let's take a look in the bedroom."
Narrator:	"So, the Bear Family climbed up the stairs to their bedroom with Papá in front. The blanket from Papá Bear's bed was on the floor."
Papá Oso:	"Mira, look at this; I KNOW I made my bed this morning . . . SOMEONE has been sleeping in MY bed!"

Mamá Osa:	"You are right Papá, and look at THIS; someone has been sleeping in MY bed too, and it's a mess!"
Osita Bebé	"Mira, Papá, Mamá, someone has been sleeping my MY bed, and HERE SHE IS!"
Narrator:	"Well, the Bears were yelling so loudly, that Curlylocks woke up with a START! "
Curlylocks:	"HELP, HELP, HELP, I'm being attacked by ferocious, wild bears."
Mamá Osa:	"Don't be silly Chiquitita, we are city bears! We are just so surprised that you would walk into our home, eat our tortillas, and then nap in our beds.
Papá Oso:	"And you know, Chiquitita, you really should not do things like this. Didn't your Mamá tell you not to wander around Prospect Park alone? Didn't she tell you NOT to talk to strangers and strange bears? You are just VERY lucky that we are nice, friendly, city bears."
Osita Bebé	"Please, Papá, don't scare my new friend. What's your name? Where did you come from? I'm Niña, and this is Mamá Osa, and Papá Oso."
Curlylocks:	"Nice to meet you. My name is Curlylocks, and I came from Mexico. Now, I live next to Prospect Park in an apartment with my mamá, and papá, and my abuela. I went for a walk to meet some new friends to play with who speak my language."
Narrator:	"Just then, Curlylocks realized that she had found a new little friend, and two large bears to talk to!"
Curlylocks:	"WAIT a minute, we are all speaking to each other! How do you know Spanish?"
Osita Bebé	"Curlylocks, we are Colorado bears, and our second language is Spanish! We are what you would call SLLs, Spanish Language Learners."
Curlylocks:	But Papá Oso, if Spanish is your second language, and English is your third language, what is your first language?"
Papá Oso:	"Well, Chiquitita, it is Bear of course!"
Curlylocks:	"Can you teach me to speak Bear too?"
Papá Oso:	"First things first, let us help you learn English, THEN we can think about learning to speak Bear."
Curlylocks:	"Well, I hope I can learn to speak English as well as Niña speaks Spanish."
Osita Bebé	"Well, since we are Colorado bears, and we have worked hard to learn Spanish and then English, we do speak three languages."

Curlylocks:	"My Mama says that I will learn English at school this year. My teachers do not understand me. I don't say much."
Osita Bebé	"Oh Curlylocks, it took a long time for me to learn too, but if you listen, and you are not afraid to make a mistake, you will learn fast! I will practice with you. Would you like that?"
Curlylocks:	"Oh yes! Can we practice next Saturday? You can come to mi casa and we can play together."
Curlylocks:	"I'm sorry about the tortillas. [Big sigh] The chicken just smelled so good, and I was so hungry, I forgot my manners, and ate your tortillas. AND then, I ate so much that I was too tired to walk home, and I fell asleep right here in Niña's bed. Here Niña, let me make your bed. I'll fix it all up for you."
Papá Oso:	"Well Miss Curlylocks . . ."
Narrator:	". . . growled Papá Bear who was very strict. He really didn't like surprises."
Papá Oso:	"Since you have already eaten Niña's tortilla, we will have to warm up MORE tortillas. Then we can all sit down together, eat our lunch, and get to know each other."
Osita Bebé	"Si. You can stay and try Papá's special Flan de Coco, with a glass of milk and honey for dessert!"
Curlylocks:	"Papá Osa, I think you must make the BEST Quesadillas in Brooklyn. And, I LOVE Flan."
Narrator:	"Curlylocks and the Brooklyn Bears had a wonderful lunch. They agreed to meet NEXT Saturday, so that Niña and Curlylocks could play together and practice speaking English. The Bears promised to go to Curlylocks' apartment for lunch." "As Curlylocks skipped home, she thought . . ."
Curlylocks:	"I cannot wait to tell my family that the Brooklyn Bears are coming for lunch next Saturday. I hope that bears like to eat 'Arroz y Frijoles' . . ."
Narrator:	"And, this was JUST the beginning of a beautiful friendship!"
Narrator:	"Now all of you children out there . . . remember, don't go walking in the park alone without a grownup, and think twice about talking to strange bears!

. . . THE END

Appendix B

Puppet Construction and Resources

EXAMPLES OF EASY-TO-CREATE PUPPETS

Patterns and detailed instructions for just about any type of puppet can be found in the library, craft books, and on the Internet. The following is a short list of those appropriate for children to create with minimal assistance.

- Finger Puppets
- Paper Plate Puppets
- Stick Puppets
- Paper Bag Puppets
- Hand Puppets with Papier Mache Heads
- Hand Puppets with Foam Heads
- Sock Puppets
- Foam-body Puppets
- Simple Marionettes

MULTICULTURAL PUPPET RESOURCES

http://www.lakeshorelearning.com/home/home.jsp
http://www.thefind.com/family/info-multicultural-puppets

PUPPET THEATERS

Patterns and detailed instructions for just about any type of puppet theater can be found in the library, craft books, and sites on the Internet. The following is a short list of those appropriate for children to create with minimal assistance.

- Table Top—Sheet Drape to hide puppeteers
- Small Box stage to sit on table top
- Poster Triptych—3-fold display- cut stage in centerfold
- Cardboard Box
- Refrigerator Box
- Folding Screen Theater
- Hollow Doors hinged together with performance windows
- Theaters may be constructed recreating various cultural situations, settings and environments.

Index

About the Authors

Giselle B. Esquivel is a Professor in the School Psychology Program of the Division of Psychological and Educational Services, Graduate School of Education at Fordham University. She is a licensed psychologist and a nationally certified school psychologist. She holds national certification in the American Board of Professional Psychology (ABPP) and is a Fellow of the American Psychological Association (APA) and the American Academy of School Psychology (AASP). Dr. Esquivel is nationally recognized for her expertise in multicultural school psychology and giftedness and creativity in culturally diverse children. She has published extensively in the above areas. Her current areas of research include positive psychology, resilience, narratives, and spirituality among children and adolescents. She serves as consulting editor, associate editor, and editorial reviewer in school psychology and APA journals.

Geraldine V. Oades-Sese is an Assistant Professor at the Graduate School of Applied and Professional Psychology of Rutgers University. She is a nationally certified school psychologist and is the founder and director of the Research Center for Resilience and Early Childhood Development and a university-based research clinic called the CREATE (Childhood Resilience & Early Achievement Toward Excellence) Clinic. Her professional experiences include providing assessment and intervention services for gifted children, as well as developmentally delayed, multiply-handicapped, and medically-fragile infants, children, and adolescents. She has authored a number of published book chapters in the *Handbook of Multicultural School Psychology, Handbook of Multicultural Assessment,* and *The Praeger Handbook of Special Education.* Her research on resilience among at-risk, culturally and linguistically diverse preschool children was published in the *Annals of the*

New York Academy of Sciences: Resilience in Children and presented at the New York Academy of Sciences, the Early Childhood Conference, APA, and at the 2008 National Association of School Psychologists (NASP) Convention on Resilience.

Marguerite L. Jarvis holds BFA from Douglass College, and a Master of Education degree from Rutgers University's Graduate School of Education. Currently, she writes and edits for educational publishers, develops websites, practices puppetry, and teaches Kindergarten. A licensed elementary school teacher, she has taught and worked with Special Needs Populations and ELL students of all ages, for more than 30 years. Peg's "Hands-On Puppets" repertory puppet company, provides puppet shows and events for schools, libraries, family, and friends. Her puppets, storytelling, and puppet-making skills continue to make literature come alive for "kids" of all ages.

Breinigsville, PA USA
30 June 2010
240925BV00002B/4/P